MW01012203

PRAISE FOR
DEMOGRAPHIC DECEPTION

"Rational optimists are history's heroes. They accurately identify credible threats, and then lead us to overcome those threats by focusing on solutions. In *Demographic Deception*, Whitney makes it clear that we have very different population challenges than we think. And then he guides us to pragmatic solutions and a bright future."

—Bert Jacobs
Co-founder and CEO, The Life is Good Company

"In *Demographic Deception*, Whitney raises an incredibly important issue for the future of the world economy. Then he asks the right questions—what does a decreasing world population mean for labor and capital markets and, ultimately, economic growth and inequality? I hope this book gets our society to start the process of getting to the answers."

—Geoffrey Sanzenbacher, PhD
Associate professor of the practice, Boston College, Department of Economics

"Whitney's *Demographic Deception* does a surgical dive into the veins of demographics and challenges the status quo to evoke discussion and discourse to ensure the future of nations and global economies."

—Kris Meyer

Hollywood producer, CEO, MuddHouse Media

"Like that memorable college professor who's teaching style makes crystal clear even the most convoluted subject matter, Dustin Whitney debunks with surgical precision the myth of overpopulation. His passion for this is contagious, and he does it with an alluring conversational style that makes the material not only digestible, but quite appetizing in the traditionally confusing and dry world of demographic data. Unafraid to take on this rhetoric that there are too many humans, he comprehensively educates the reader on this topic about which few of us know much and explains to us how and why we should know more."

—Jason Fanuele, MD

Assistant professor, The Warren Alpert Medical School, Brown University

"Dustin Whitney looks at a global trend that will have distinct local implications. A future of declining population challenges common strategies about competing for people and talent to build stronger communities and economies. Whitney's work will give anyone interested in stronger communities and economic development some fresh perspectives on how to approach the future."

—Peter Forman
President and CEO, Chamber of commerce, SSMA

"*Demographic Deception* is a very thought-provoking book that shines an honest, common sense light on the forces of ignorance and deceit manipulating society. Dustin Whitney takes a careful approach, using compelling good news/bad news segments, in debunking the myths about generational divides promoted by special interests. This fascinating material underscores the need for open public debate to counterbalance the deceit and ensure the best possible future outcome.

Demographic Deception deserves to be shared widely as an illuminating guidebook to help leaders and citizens re-think establishment groupthink and secure our shared destiny. I cannot wait to buy copies for others who will benefit from Whitney's urgent wakeup call."

—Spencer Collier
CEO, getfused

DEMOGRAPHIC DECEPTION

DUSTIN WHITNEY

DEMOGRAPHIC DECEPTION

Exposing the Overpopulation Myth and Building a Resilient Future

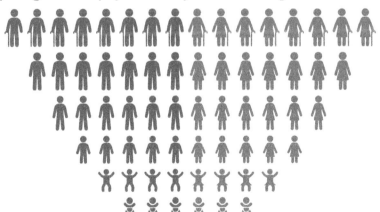

Advantage | Books

Published by Advantage Books, Charleston, South Carolina.
An imprint of Advantage Media.

ADVANTAGE is a registered trademark, and the Advantage colophon is a trademark of Advantage Media Group, Inc.

Printed in the United States of America.

10 9 8 7 6 5 4 3 2 1

ISBN: 978-1-64225-817-2 (Hardcover)
ISBN: 978-1-64225-816-5 (eBook)

Library of Congress Control Number: 2023917037

Cover and layout design by Analisa Smith.

This publication is designed to provide accurate and authoritative information in regard to the subject matter covered. It is sold with the understanding that the publisher is not engaged in rendering legal, accounting, or other professional services. If legal advice or other expert assistance is required, the services of a competent professional person should be sought.

Advantage Books is an imprint of Advantage Media Group. Advantage Media helps busy entrepreneurs, CEOs, and leaders write and publish a book to grow their business and become the authority in their field. Advantage authors comprise an exclusive community of industry professionals, idea-makers, and thought leaders. For more information go to **advantagemedia.com**.

To Rick,
my dear friend and mentor.

Knowing yourself is the beginning of all wisdom.
—ARISTOTLE

CONTENTS

INTRODUCTION

I n the fall of 2022, demographers at the United Nations estimated that the global human population had officially reached eight billion people on November 15.[1] Headline after headline bellowed a narrative that most of us already believed: our numbers were spiraling out of control, threatening the health of our planet and everything on it. But just two days later, on November 17, there was another headline—this one in *Fortune*—that told quite a different story: "The World's Baby Shortfall Is So Bad That the Labor Shortage Will Last for Years, Major Employment Firms Predict."[2]

How could it be that our population was spiraling out of control if a "baby shortfall" had caused a labor shortage—one that many of us were already starting to feel—that would last for years?

This was a question I'd been asking myself for a while—ever since a conversation a few years back that I'd had with a mentor of mine who is heavily involved in the Catholic Church. He was telling me about recent efforts to bolster declining church attendance, and from there our talk drifted to the topic of decreasing birth rates.

I'll be honest—I'd never thought much about birth or fertility rates. But for whatever reason, that discussion with my mentor stayed with me. I started noticing things that seemed to relate to fertility rates and, more broadly, shifting population trends. I read about labor shortages in Canada and abandoned villages in Europe. I watched news reports on the high proportion of elderly people in Japan. Closer to home, in Hingham, Massachusetts, I saw fewer and fewer children playing in our parks and noticed that exactly zero of the younger women on my staff—at least at that time—had kids.

None of these observations squared with the prevailing view that our planet was in danger of being overpopulated. It got me curious. *What was going on?*

I'm a numbers guy. Always have been. So I began digging into whatever data I could find. I started with data from the United Nations Population Division (UNPD)—the foremost source of global population data and forecasts. Pretty soon I was swimming in data. The deeper I got, the more I felt like things just weren't adding up.

What really caught my attention was a discrepancy between projected fertility trends and actual ones. Shockingly, population modelers had not accurately predicted fertility rates for decades. In many areas fertility rates had fallen much faster and were now much lower than the UNPD had projected. These trends would inevitably affect population numbers down the line, and yet it seemed that the UNPD's population forecasts ignored them. As a result I believed their population projections were too high. More specifically I believed the populations of most advanced economies would age and decline much sooner than anticipated, and that peak population would occur much earlier, and at a much lower number, than previously supposed.

This got me worried. Governments, nongovernmental organizations (NGOs), businesses, nonprofits, and even private individuals use population forecasts generated by the UNPD for planning and risk management purposes, and if I'd done my math right, those forecasts were wrong. This meant that in the years to come, these entities would be making extremely consequential decisions—around infrastructure, public services, education, health, research and development, business practices and investments, and more—based on flawed facts. The results could be disastrous (not to mention costly), upending every assumption we have about the future.

I was worried about something else too. If these forecasts were wrong, then many countries were about to experience aging and even declining populations much sooner than expected. Some countries already had. (Recall my mention of the high proportion of elderly people in Japan.) Aging and declining populations bring a host of problems, which, for the sake of brevity, I will summarize here as too few workers, producing too few goods and services, and various cascading economic and societal effects.

I didn't know what to do. I mean, I wasn't 100 percent certain my analysis was correct. After all, I'm not a demographer; I'm in business. I started my career during the mid-1990s growing and developing small- to medium-sized companies. These days I run my own organization, the Whitney Group. We operate at the intersection of design and innovation to help entrepreneurs start and grow companies and to help more advanced companies build resilience and longevity. There was another reason for my hesitation, though: I was on the tail end of a decade-long personal journey during which I had by necessity adopted a pretty powerful sense of humility. So I knew better than to barge into a discussion about a topic in which I was admittedly not (yet) an expert, like I had all the answers.

Still, I felt unsettled. That same personal journey had imbued in me a powerful sense of concern for our planet and the people in it and, more importantly, a duty to take action to make the world a better place. I thought a lot about the society my kids would inherit. I didn't want their generation, and the generations that followed, to bear the burden of our failures today, especially since, if the population did indeed decline, there would be fewer people to shoulder it. The spread of COVID-19 in early 2020 and subsequent chaos only added to my sense of responsibility and the need to act.

Then something interesting happened: in July 2020 a couple of competing organizations issued their own population projections, and those projections aligned a lot more closely with mine. Boy, was I relieved! I thought this development would prompt *everyone* to reevaluate their assumptions about population trends.

Well, they didn't. This was made abundantly clear to me in April 2022 when I attended a major conference on population trends. It was the first such meeting of population scientists since the start of the pandemic, and the world's top demographers were in attendance: scholars from universities, think tanks, NGOs, and organizations such as the United Nations (UN) and the World Bank. Rather than carefully considering the analyses put forth by those competing organizations—one of which had been funded by the highly reputable Gates Foundation—they mocked them.

I found this shocking. Regardless of which projections might ultimately be more accurate, the outright dismissal of these analyses struck me as unwarranted. Something else struck me too: of the 236 sessions, only a few of them even *mentioned* declining fertility rates. And virtually none of them discussed issues around labor and economics. Global banking policy, inflationary controls, gross domestic product (GDP)—all these are predicated on labor markets. It seemed very unusual to not explore or even acknowledge the obvious connections between population trends and the labor force, especially when countries all over the world were already experiencing labor shortages in the wake of the COVID-19 pandemic.

I'm still not a demographer. But now I believe that might be a good thing. I mean absolutely zero disrespect when I say this, but I worry that demography as a discipline has become entrenched in its approach and its point of view. As an outsider maybe I can offer a different and more holistic assessment. That's why, after much soul-searching and internal debate, I wrote this book.

My objectives here are simple. First, I want to exhort readers to question the prevailing narrative that our planet is hopelessly over-populated and that we as a species are doomed to destruction. This narrative is not just false; it's deceptive. Second, I want to inform people about the possible effects—some good and some bad—of plummeting fertility rates, aging societies, and population decline all over the world. Finally, I want to initiate a conversation about how we might evade a *real* looming demographic disaster, in which human populations and individuals fail to flourish.

My hope is to convince as many leaders and innovators as possible to take immediate action to avert what could otherwise amount to a global crisis. The sooner we plan, innovate, and adapt, the less disruptive and painful these coming changes will be. Indeed, if we play our cards right, they could even present some opportunities.

None of this can occur if we don't first acknowledge and understand what's happening now. We *must* recognize what's going on. The facts are there. The numbers are playing out right before our eyes. It's up to us to see them. It's up to us to act.

CHAPTER 1

THE MALTHUSIAN NIGHTMARE

The power of the population is indefinitely greater than the power in the earth to produce subsistence for man.

—THOMAS R. MALTHUS, AUTHOR OF *AN ESSAY ON THE PRINCIPLE OF POPULATION*

For nearly all of human history, spanning more than two million years, our experience on earth has been defined by our struggle to survive. Early hominids faced all manner of threats—predation, starvation, disease, wounds, exposure, weather events, climate change, violence, and war.

For our Paleolithic predecessors, life was, as described by seventeenth-century English philosopher Thomas Hobbes, "solitary, poor, nasty, brutish, and short."[3] The average life expectancy was just twenty-two years.[4] Roughly 30 percent of all babies born during prehistoric and ancient times perished before their first birthday, and fewer than half reached reproductive age.[5]

> **NOTE:** The high infant and child mortality rate helps explain the short average life span of early humans. Those lucky few who lived to adulthood might reasonably expect to survive to the age of fifty or perhaps sixty. Some people even lived into their eighties.

The tenuous nature of our survival drove our mastery of fire, our invention of tools and weapons, our transition from clans of hunter-gatherers to agrarian collectives to complex civilizations, our development of language and letters, and our discovery of scientific and medical phenomena. Each of these crucial advancements lengthened our lives and increased our numbers.

Our fragile existence also inspired a preoccupation with fertility and birth. Archaeologists believe that some of the earliest examples of prehistoric art were fertility charms—statuettes called *Venus figurines* that date back as far as 35,000 BCE. Fertility deities also populated the pantheons of many primeval polytheistic religions, including those practiced by the Phoenicians, Sumerians, Egyptians, Greeks, Romans, Indians, Aztecs, and Chinese. And of course, in the very first chapter of the Hebrew Bible, or Old Testament, the Judeo-Christian god exhorts Adam and Eve (and presumably the rest of us) to "be fruitful and multiply."

EARLY HUMAN POPULATION GROWTH

Our earliest forebears did multiply. But how much, and how quickly, is largely an exercise in educated guesswork, at least until the Paleolithic and Mesolithic periods yielded to the Neolithic period roughly twelve thousand years ago.

NOTE: The Paleolithic and Mesolithic periods were character-ized by nomadic hunter-gatherer societies and the use of crude stone tools. During the Neolithic period, rudimentary farming and animal-husbandry practices emerged, allowing for the proliferation of more permanent settlements.

Paleo-demographers estimate that around 10,000 BCE, the total human population—which by then had spread from Africa, where our earliest ancestors emerged, all over the globe—was between 1 and 10 million people. By 5000 BCE, as civilizations sprouted in the Indus and Tigris-Euphrates valleys, the total human population was perhaps between 5 and 20 million. From 1000 BCE to 1 CE—during which complex and advanced societies flourished in Greece, Rome, China, and Japan; throughout Africa and in Mesoamerica; and across the Levant—it climbed from 50 million (1000 BCE) to 100 million (500 BCE) to between 170 million and 400 million (1 CE), depending on who's counting.[6]

The UN, widely seen as the authority on population numbers in general, estimates that the actual population at the time of Christ was 300 million people.[7] If that number is accurate, it means our population grew by a factor of eight in the millennium spanning 1000 BCE and 1 CE. The next thousand years, however, told a somewhat different story. The global population continued to grow but more slowly, perhaps because of the slow-moving fracture of the Roman Empire in the first half of that period and Western Europe's sub-sequent descent into the Dark Ages. UN estimates put the human population in the year 1000 CE at 310 million—just 10 million more than in 1 CE.[8] Some experts, such as French demographer Jean-Noël

Biraben, have suggested that our population actually *declined* during this period to 254 million.[9]

Child mortality remained the primary impediment to human flourishing. Not even members of royalty were spared. During the thirteenth century, King Edward I of England and his wife Queen Eleanor welcomed sixteen children. Of these, ten died in childhood, and only three lived past the age of forty. These children "enjoyed the best conditions and the most nurturing surroundings that could be provided in medieval Europe," writes Yuval Noah Harari in *Sapiens: A Brief History of Humankind.* "They lived in palaces, ate as much food as they liked, had plenty of warm clothing, well-stocked fireplaces, the cleanest water available, an army of servants and the best doctors."[10] But still, they died.

According to Biraben, the human population surged to 443 million around 1340.[11] But the bubonic plague, or Black Death, disrupted this upward trajectory. The disease emerged first in China in 1323, where it exterminated 40 percent of the population. By 1346 it had snaked the Silk Road to Crimea. From there it swarmed Eurasia, North Africa, and Europe, before eventually petering out in 1353. This pestilence, spread initially by fleas and later person-to-person, killed as many as 200 million denizens of the Old World. Some 25 million people perished from the plague in Europe alone, between 30 and 60 percent of that continent's population, with urban areas being particularly hard hit. Indeed, more than a century passed before European numbers returned to preplague levels.

The indigenous people of North America fared even worse after European explorers alit on their shores in the late 1400s. Nearly 90 percent of that population died in the century after Christopher Columbus moored in the Bahamas in 1492. "War, slavery and wave after wave of disease combined to cause this 'great dying,' something the world had never seen before, or since," say scholars Mark Maslin and Simon Lewis.[12]

Even under the best circumstances, observe Marian L. Tupy and Gale L. Pooley in their book *Superabundance,*

> people lacked basic medicines and died relatively young. They had no painkillers, and people with ailments spent much of their lives in agonizing pain. Entire families lived in bug-infested dwellings that offered neither comfort nor privacy. They worked in the fields from sunrise to sunset, yet hunger and famines were commonplace. Transportation was primitive, and most people never traveled beyond their native villages or nearest towns. Ignorance and illiteracy were ubiquitous.[13]

All this is to say that for various reasons, from the dawn of humankind until roughly the Renaissance, humankind just barely survived. Our numbers grew slowly, if they grew at all.

THOMAS MALTHUS AND THE "DISMAL SCIENCE"

According to UN estimates, the global population surpassed 500 million around 1500.[14] So it took more than ten thousand years for our numbers to grow from between 1 million and 10 million to half a billion. The next half billion people arrived much more quickly. In just three hundred years, our population doubled, reaching 1 billion sometime around 1800.

This explosive growth was due in large part to scientific discoveries. In particular, advancements in medicine and sanitation improved living conditions, reduced infant mortality rates, and prolonged lives.

At last, our species was doing more than merely surviving. It was succeeding beyond our early ancestors' wildest imaginings!

For British economist and cleric Thomas Malthus, our growing global population was a cause not for celebration but alarm. He believed the earth could not sustain these increasing numbers. He published a treatise on the subject in 1798: *An Essay on the Principle of Population*. The main thesis of this treatise was that "[t]he power of the population is indefinitely greater than the power in the earth to produce subsistence for man." In other words, at some point, it would be impossible to produce enough food to feed the human population.

This explosive growth was due in large part to scientific discoveries. In particular, advancements in medicine and sanitation improved living conditions, reduced infant mortality rates, and prolonged lives.

The obvious answer to this problem would be to develop new ways to improve farming yields. But Malthus preferred another solution: "All children born, beyond what would be required to keep up the population to a desired level, must necessarily perish, unless room be made for them by the deaths of grown persons."[15]

Malthus supposed this would happen organically. He believed that as human numbers increased, poverty and misery would increase in kind. This would naturally cull the population and thereby maintain its balance. (He considered this a "positive" check.) Malthus even warned against assisting the indigent because it would inhibit this natural culling. (Besides, he said, "Dependent poverty ought to be held disgraceful."[16]) He also discouraged efforts to improve human health—for example, through sanitation and vaccines—writing in his 1798 treatise,

> Instead of recommending cleanliness to the poor, we should encourage contrary habits. In our towns we should make the streets narrower, crowd more people into the houses, and court the return of the plague. In the country, we should build our villages near stagnant pools, and particularly encourage settlements in all marshy and unwholesome situations. But above all, we should reprobate specific remedies for ravaging diseases; and restrain those benevolent, but much mistaken men, who have thought they were doing a service to mankind by projecting schemes for the total extirpation of particular disorders.[17]

NOTE: The pessimistic nature of Malthus's views, which are believed to have inspired the character Ebenezer Scrooge in Charles Dickens's *A Christmas Carol*, moved his contemporaries to dub economics the "dismal science."

Malthus was wrong about our inability to accommodate a growing human population. In the years since Malthus published his essay, the earth's population has octupled in size. And although there is indeed misery and poverty, these are not due to our planet's inability to "produce subsistence," as Malthus put it, but rather to humankind's failure to distribute it effectively. "Famines still occur," say Tupy and Pooley, "but they are becoming more rare and now are always the result of bad economic policies or war."[18] Still, as radical and pitiless as it was, Malthusianism has remained both popular and influential, particularly in times of want.

MALTHUS, DARWINISM, AND EUGENICS

The Malthusian notion that spiraling population growth would pit people against each other, with some living and some dying, informed Charles Darwin's thinking on the subject of natural selection. Darwin's articulation of natural selection in turn inspired his cousin Francis Galton to apply it to the selective breeding of human beings so that "humanity shall be represented by the fittest races"[19] (meaning Anglo-Saxon and Nordic people). Galton called this practice *eugenics*, meaning "good stock" or "wellborn."

Eugenics was "the face of population control in the first half of the twentieth century," says Fred Pearce, author of *The Coming Population Crash*.[20] Several countries enacted laws to legalize eugenic practices. Some of these laws were intended to prevent certain members of society (such as the mentally ill) from marrying and to outlaw interracial marriage. Others called for the sterilization of "unfit" people. In Germany, eugenics, specifically the notion of a "master race," was the philosophical foundation of the Nazi regime and the Holocaust "an extreme expression of a more general eugenics movement," says Pearce.[21]

Today eugenics is widely rejected. But a recent surge in white supremacism has given rise to a new variation on eugenics: White Replacement Theory.

"This theory," says journalist Dave Saldana, "has its foundation in the fact that homogenous populations cannot exist undisturbed for long—that is, a 'pure race' can only be maintained by rigid exclusion of any outsiders, which is ultimately impossible." Therefore, argue adherents of the White Replacement Theory, "'Outsiders' must be subjugated, exiled, or eliminated."[22]

Needless to say, White Replacement Theory, like all strains of eugenics, is wholly unacceptable and should have no place in modern society.

THE TWENTIETH CENTURY

Recall that it took three hundred years for the global population to double from 500 million to 1 billion. The next doubling occurred in less than half that time. Even after the unthinkable loss of life in the American Civil War (1861–1865), the Boer War (1899–1902), the Russo-Japanese War (1904–1905), the Great War (1914–1918), the Armenian Genocide (1915–1917), the Russian Revolution (1917) and subsequent famine (1921), and the influenza epidemic (1918), the human population reached 2 billion around 1927.[23]

The next billion people came even faster. Despite the staggering human deaths associated with the Stalinization of Russia (including the Holodomor in Ukraine) during the 1930s, World War II and the Holocaust (1939–1945), America's deployment of the atomic bomb in Japan (1945), the Korean War (1950–1953), the Vietnam War (1955–1975), and Mao Zedong's "Great Leap Forward" (1958–1962), the human population reached 3 billion sometime around 1960 and 4 billion in 1974.[24]

Global population growth after World War II was "quantitatively and qualitatively different from any previous epoch in human history," said a classified memorandum issued by the US National Security Agency in 1974. The memorandum, popularly referred to as the "Kissinger Report" (after then National Security Advisor Henry Kissinger), continued, "Total growth rates are close to 2 percent a year, compared with about 1 percent before World War II, under 0.5 percent in 1750–1900, and far lower rates before 1750."[25] This memorandum, which remained classified until 1989, would inform various aspects of US government policy for decades.

Because of the plunge in infant mortality, the average human life span increased.

One explanation for this surge in the human population was the baby boom (1946–1964)—a product of soldiers returning home from World War II who "celebrated peace by starting families," says Pearce.[26] Between 1946 and 1964, more than 72 million babies were born in the United States alone;[27] in 1964 the global fertility rate peaked at 5.1 children per woman.[28]

Even more significant was that breakthroughs in medicine and public health, most notably the invention of penicillin and other lifesaving antibiotics as well as several vaccines, ensured that the vast majority of infants survived to reproductive age. So it wasn't just that people had more babies; more (almost all!) of those babies survived.

Because of the plunge in infant mortality, the average human life span increased. But it increased for another reason too: thanks to those same advancements in medicine and public health, people who reached adulthood lived longer than their forebears. Ultimately, according to a 2002 *Scientific American* report, "Rapid declines in infant, child, maternal and late-life mortality during the 20th century led to an unprecedented 30-year increase in human life expectancy at birth [to 77 years] from the 47 years that it was in developed countries in 1900."[29]

> **NOTE:** These improvements heralded particularly dramatic population growth in the developing world. After World War II, Indonesia doubled its population in thirty-one years, Nigeria in twenty-eight years, Turkey and Kenya in twenty-four years, Brazil in twenty-two years, the Philippines in twenty years, El Salvador in nineteen years, and Costa Rica in seventeen years.[30]

"THE POPULATION BOMB"

The surging global population during the mid-twentieth century sparked a revival of Malthusianism. Two books on this topic were particularly influential: *Our Plundered Planet* (1948) by Henry Fairfield Osborn Jr. and *Road to Survival* (1948) by William Vogt. Both warned of imminent environmental devastation because of what Osborn described as a "violent upsurge in human numbers."[31]

"The tide of the earth's population is rising and the reservoir of the earth's living resources is falling,"[32] cautioned Osborn. Vogt agreed. "The earth is not made of rubber," he wrote. "It cannot be stretched; the human race, every nation, is limited in the number of acres it possesses. And as the number of human beings increases, the relative amount of productive earth decreases, by that amount." Vogt even went as far as to assert that ecological collapse would trigger nuclear war as countries clawed for resources. "When this comes," he wrote, "it is probable that at least three-quarters of the human race will be wiped out."[33]

Vogt's book struck a chord with American businessman Hugh Everett Moore, founder of the Dixie Cup Company. In 1954 Moore published his own views on the topic in a pamphlet called "The Population Bomb." Its key message: "The population bomb threatens to create an explosion as disruptive and dangerous as the explosion of the atom, and with as much influence on prospects for progress or disaster, war or peace."[34] Moore was particularly concerned that population growth in certain areas could influence the outcome of the Cold War. "We are not primarily interested in the sociological or humanitarian aspects of birth control," he noted. "We are interested in the use which Communists make of hungry people in their drive to conquer the earth."[35]

In 1968 a Stanford University biology professor named Dr. Paul R. Ehrlich published a controversial book in the same vein and with the same title as Moore's pamphlet: *The Population Bomb*. (Ehrlich coauthored the book with his wife, Anne, whose work went uncredited at the time.) The book, which would sell more than three million copies, was positively apocalyptic, from its very opening paragraph:

> The battle to feed all of humanity is over. In the 1970's, the world will undergo famines—hundreds of millions of people are going to starve to death in spite of any crash programs embarked upon now. At this late date nothing can prevent a substantial increase in the world death rate.[36]

NOTE: Thanks to his provocative tone and his penetration into popular culture—he appeared on *The Tonight Show Starring Johnny Carson* more than a dozen times—Ehrlich moved the discussion of overpopulation from academic circles to the general public.

Another publication, *A Blueprint for Survival*, released in 1973 by Edward Goldsmith and cosigned by more than thirty leading scientists, reinforced Ehrlich's message:

> If current trends are allowed to persist, the breakdown of society and the irreversible disruption of the life-support systems on this planet, possibly by the end of the century, certainly within the lifetimes of our children, are inevitable.[37]

These dire predictions did not come to pass. Hundreds of millions of people did not die of hunger in the 1970s. Society remains intact, and our planet lives on. But the overall message of these publications seeped into our collective consciousness. It's one reason so many of us today believe that our planet is hopelessly overpopulated.

The notion of overpopulation has even entered the modern zeitgeist. It was the major theme of the hit Marvel Studios movie *Avengers: Infinity War*, in which (spoiler alert) a billionaire alien warlord (Thanos) seeks to eliminate half of all living things to stabilize the universe's population and resources. Similarly, in the 2016 movie *Inferno*, a billionaire scientist (again, spoiler alert) develops a virus to randomly sterilize one-third of the human population. And in the 2014 film *Kingsman: The Secret Service*, a billionaire ecoterrorist (one more time, spoiler alert) devises a scheme to wipe out most of humanity to avert climate catastrophe. (What is it with these billionaires?)

EIGHT BILLION AND COUNTING

Since the publication of *The Population Bomb* in 1968, the global population has soared. The UN estimates it reached 8 billion in November 2022. (See fig. 1.1.) That is a big number indeed. And our population will continue to grow (although how much, and for how long, is up for debate).

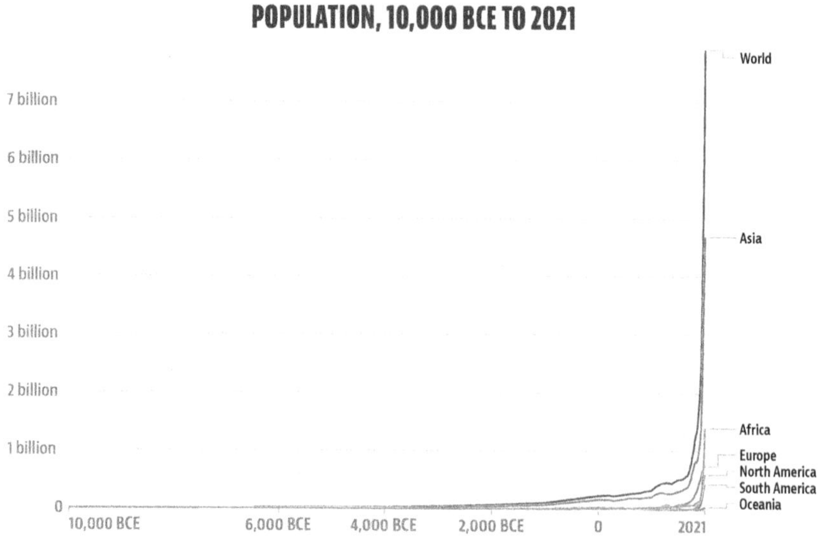

POPULATION, 10,000 BCE TO 2021

Figure 1.1. Global population numbers from 10,000 BCE to 2021 (Source: Our World in Data)

One can perhaps see why Ehrlich stated in 2018 that "a shattering collapse of civilization … is a near certainty in the next few decades."[38] Our awareness of climate change, which has accelerated in tandem with our growing population, naturally heightens our concern. Indeed, many see overpopulation as "the unspoken driver of environmental destruction,"[39] says Pearce.

This attitude was evident in comments posted online about a recent TED Talk by Wajahat Ali that made the case for having

CHAPTER 1: THE MALTHUSIAN NIGHTMARE

children. "The population of the world has tripled in the last hundred years. We don't need more. Time to slow down, reduce pressure on planetary resources, and make sure there's enough water and food for everyone that is already here," one commentator wrote. "Humans are the worst thing to happen to this beautiful planet. Unless we can overcome our greed, selfishness, and lack of respect for nature and the climate, which is never going to happen, the best thing for Earth would be for all the humans to die off. #stopreproducing,"[40] wrote another.

Not everyone shares this view, of course. Some scholars have adopted a more optimistic stance. They're called *cornucopianists*, after the magical horn of plenty in Greek mythology. They refute the Malthusian tenet that unchecked population growth inevitably results in misery. After all, they say, the global population has effectively quadrupled just in the last century, and yet by any objective measure—living standards, longevity, health, wealth, opportunities—most of us are better off than our ancestors.

And while most people see the earth's resources as finite, cornucopians, who often identify as libertarians, disagree. They believe that as one resource grows scarce, humans inevitably find or invent a better, more abundant one to replace it, the way iron replaced bronze when tin became scarce around 1200 BCE, coal replaced timber in the 1500s, oil dug from the earth replaced whale oil in the 1800s, and fiber-optic cable replaced copper wires during our own lifetimes. Some, like cornucopian economist Julian Simon, have even gone as far as to suggest the more humans, the better, calling human ingenuity the "ultimate resource." (More on that in chapter 6.)

So which side is right? Will an ever-growing population overwhelm our environment and prevent us from sustaining ourselves, as so many people seem to think? Or, to quote Pearce, will having "more hands to work and brains to think … more than compensate for the extra mouths to feed?"[41]

I don't have the answer. And in any case, I believe the question is moot. Ultimately, I believe the global population will *not* continue to grow unchecked. I think it will decline—quickly, precipitously, and soon. And when it does, we'll need to be ready.

CHAPTER 2

A PRIMER ON POPULATION MODELING

The determinants of population growth are not well understood, especially for low income societies.

—THE KISSINGER REPORT

P opulation modeling is all about predicting whether the size of a given population is likely to change. If the answer is yes (spoiler alert: it always is), then the goal of population modeling shifts to forecasting when that change is likely to occur and how significant that change will be.

As you might imagine, this is a complex and imperfect operation, so much so it might be reasonable to ask whether it's really worth doing at all. That's the purpose of this chapter: to explain why population modeling is important and how it works. It also addresses other issues pertaining to population modeling—most notably, that the various entities that perform population modeling often produce vastly different projections.

THE IMPORTANCE OF POPULATION MODELING

Predicting when a population might change, and by how much, is no easy exercise. So why do it? The answer is simple: governments and NGOs, businesses and nonprofits, and even private individuals use population forecasts, however imprecise they may be, for planning and risk management purposes.

Let's focus on governments because the plans and policies implemented by these entities have an outsize effect in terms of economic opportunities, quality of life, and social stability. "Every government is interested in what is going to happen to their population in the next couple of decades, for pragmatic economic reasons and planning needs," says population researcher Tomáš Sobotka.[42] For example, governments need short-term and mid-term population projections to

- estimate how many schools, hospitals, post offices, airports, and other structures they need to build or maintain;

- determine what types of public services they'll have to support;

- inform future investments in infrastructure, such as bridges and roads, public transportation, energy grids, and so on;

- identify what skills and knowledge the next generations of workers will require; and

- decide how best to allocate resources for health research and development.[43]

In addition to short-term and mid-term population projections, governments also need long-term projections to "understand potential environmental, military, geopolitical, and other risks to implement prevention or mitigation strategies," say researchers at the Institute for Health Metrics and Evaluation (IHME).[44]

NGOs such as the UN use short-, mid-, and long-term population projections to, in the UN's words, "provide essential goods and services for the population—including food, water, energy, housing, infrastructure, health, education and social protection—as well as prospects for full employment, better living standards and reduced environmental pressure."[45]

As for businesses and individuals, they rely on population projections to make long-term decisions and investments. Individuals also use these projections, whether they know it or not, to predict their future tax burden and the likelihood of receiving pension and health benefits down the road.

If the population projections on which they rely are inaccurate, or if they're ignored altogether, the effect can be disastrous.

These are all critical decisions. If the population projections on which they rely are inaccurate, or if they're ignored altogether, the effect can be disastrous.

Here's a local example from my town, Hingham, Massachusetts. Hingham is a small town. We have four elementary schools. One of those schools, William L. Foster Elementary School, is quite outdated and in need of significant repair. There's broad support for this, and I see why. I mean, I'm an education guy. I believe in allocating robust educational resources to nurture strong foundations and build for the future. There's just one problem: *we don't need four elementary schools.*

In 2010 elementary school enrollment in Hingham was 1,785 children. In 2022 that number was 1,425. That's a decrease of more than 20 percent.[46] (Incidentally, as shown in figure 2.1, middle school and high school enrollments are also down.)

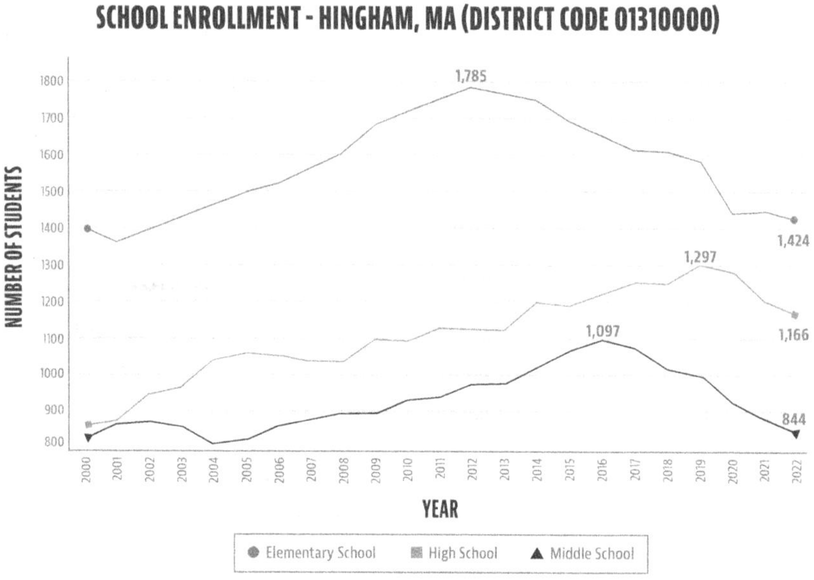

SCHOOL ENROLLMENT - HINGHAM, MA (DISTRICT CODE 01310000)

Figure 2.1. School enrollment in Hingham, Massachusetts (Source: Massachusetts Department of Education)

Hingham's under-5 set—kids who aren't yet old enough to attend school—has also contracted, from 1,565 in 2010 to 1,333 in 2022.[47] So in the next few years, even fewer kids will be enrolled in our elementary schools. Beyond that, I expect the numbers to drop even further because our town skews old. We have *way* more people aged thirty-five and up (15,657) than we do age twenty to thirty-four (1,946).[48] Sure, some people have kids in their late thirties and even into their forties, but as any good OB-GYN will tell you, those aren't prime childbearing years. There are simply going to be fewer children.

All this is to say that over the long term, three elementary schools would be more than sufficient to support the educational needs of the Hingham community *without* sacrificing quality. And yet either because they're not aware of these numbers or they're just ignoring them, city planners continue to commit tremendous resources— federal, state, and local—to rebuilding that fourth school.

> **NOTE:** Think about how many other Hinghams there are out there, across the country and around the world!

Here's another example: If you've ever spent any time in the Dallas–Fort Worth area in Texas, you've probably noticed the countless subdivisions sprawled across the region. You've also likely observed that most of the homes in these subdivisions are supersized—tons of square footage and enormous lawns.

Why are there so many, and why are they so big? Because between 2010 and 2020, the area added 1.2 million people.[49] Drawn by lucrative work opportunities, tons of these transplants have landed good jobs, make good money, and have started families. *And they're still coming.* According to an article published in April 2022 in the *Dallas Morning News*, builders in the Dallas–Fort Worth area broke ground on nearly sixteen thousand new homes in the first quarter of that year—a 4.5 percent increase from the year before.[50]

OK. Maybe all those subdivisions make sense, at least in the short term. But in the long term? Not so much. Over the next decade, population experts predict that the Dallas–Fort Worth area will shed 80,000 children under sixteen and gain more than 200,000 people over sixty-five.[51] The large suburban and exurban homes built to accommodate the influx of workers and young families won't be suitable for older people. Those properties are too big. They're hard to maintain. So demand for those gargantuan houses will likely plummet—and their prices along with it. This will be a devastating development for anyone whose long-term financial plans are based on their home equity.

Changes in population age and size have significant economic, social, environmental, and geopolitical effects.

The point is that changes in population age and size have significant economic, social, environmental, and geopolitical effects. So the models used to forecast population changes must be as accurate as possible.

FORECASTING POPULATION CHANGES

Population modelers use the following three main metrics to forecast changes in the size of a particular population:

- Fertility (birth) rate

- Mortality (death) rate

- Immigration (the movement of people to and from a region) rate

Modelers also need to know the answer to one important question: How many people are alive within that population today? With all this information in hand, modelers calculate the projected population over a set period.

DEMOGRAPHIC TRANSITION MODEL[52]

In 1929 an American demographer named Warren Thompson developed what he called the Demographic Transition Model. Its purpose was to articulate the various stages of demographic transition. Thompson defined these stages as follows:

STAGE 1: This stage is defined by high birth rates, high death rates, and limited population growth. Much of the world existed in this stage before the Industrial Revolution.

STAGE 2: In this stage, the death rate drops, especially among children, but birth rates remain high, causing a surge in population. This stage often yields what population modelers call a *demographic dividend*, defined by the United Nations Population Fund (UNFPA) as "the economic growth potential that can result from shifts in a population's age structure, mainly when the share of the working population (15 to 64) is larger than the non-working share of the population (14 and younger and 65 and older)."[53]

STAGE 3: In this stage, birth rates gradually drop while death rates remain low. The result: A population that continues to grow but more slowly. Most developing countries today are in stage 3.

STAGE 4: During this stage, birth *and* death rates are low, so population numbers remain stable. Stage 4 countries typically have a more educated populace, a stronger economy, more women in the workplace, and better healthcare.

Although Thompson conceived of only four stages, a fifth stage has since emerged. In stage 5 the death rate remains low, and the birth rate plummets below replacement levels (more on this later), resulting first in a population with more old people than young people and eventually in population decline. Many developed countries appear to be in stage 5.

CALCULATING THE CURRENT POPULATION

You probably already know the main tool by which various entities calculate the current population: the census. Essentially, a census is a head count, although modern censuses often gather additional information about a population too, such as gender, race, and so on.

Censuses are nothing new. Government officials conducted censuses in one form or another in ancient Babylonia, Palestine, Persia, China, Egypt, and Rome. In the United States, we've conducted a census every ten years since 1790, as mandated in our Constitution. This decennial process has yielded numerous innovative techniques and technological breakthroughs for gathering, analyzing, and reporting population data.

Still, the census is an imperfect instrument. It's subject to political influence, of course, like how the US census initially counted each slave as only three-fifths of a person. And in areas of the world consumed by poverty, instability, or strife, conducting a census is all but impossible. For example, the last time government officials conducted a census in the Democratic Republic of Congo was in 1984, and in Afghanistan, it was in 1979. These governments are generally left to estimate their current population by assuming a linear annual increase—an operation that's about as accurate as shaking a Magic 8 Ball.

NOTE: COVID-19 hobbled the efforts of pretty much every country to conduct their regular censuses, at least temporarily.

Fortunately, demographers and statisticians have developed clever ways to "count people without actually counting them," says David Adam at *Nature*.[54] For example, they might monitor mobile phone traffic to estimate local populations or use satellite images to gauge the size and shape of residential buildings in an attempt to estimate the number of people who live in them. However, population researcher Andy Tatem says, "These methods should be seen as a complement to the census rather than something to replace it."[55]

FERTILITY RATE

A population's total fertility rate equals the average number of live births delivered by each woman in that population during her lifetime. In population modeling the total fertility rate is a critical input. It's also the most changeable, influenced by countless societal, cultural, biological, and economic variables.

Chief among these variables is child mortality rate—that is, the number of children per one thousand live births who die before they reach age five. Generally speaking, a higher child mortality rate results in a higher fertility rate; couples conceive more children in the hopes that at least some of them will live to adulthood. Conversely, Darrell Bricker and John Ibbitson say in their book *Empty Planet*, "Parents have fewer children when they are confident those children will survive."[56]

There are other variables too. For example, women who are literate and educated tend to have fewer babies.[57] The African country of Angola provides a stark example: Angolan women "without any schooling have 7.8 children, whereas those with tertiary education have 2.3," says the *Economist*. Why? "Educated women have a better chance of a job, so the opportunity cost of staying at home to look after children."[58] The same goes for women whose work is very important to them or who enjoy the prestige associated with their job, especially in countries where "efforts to achieve gender equality" rest primarily on "the normativity of career-mindedness," say Laurie DeRose and Lyman Stone at the Institute for Family Studies.[59]

> **NOTE:** Recent research suggests that men who are educated tend to have fewer children too.[60]

Then there's urbanization. In 2007, for the first time ever, more people lived in urban areas than in rural ones, and the number of urban dwellers is likely to grow. This is significant in this context because when a population becomes urbanized, its total fertility rate drops. "On a farm, a child is an investment—an extra pair of hands to milk the cow, or shoulders to work the fields," say Bricker and Ibbitson. "But in a city, a child is a liability, just another mouth to feed." In other words, they say, "Parents who live in cities are only acting in their own economic interest by reducing the size of the litter."[61] We see this in Africa, where urban women typically have between 30 and 40 percent fewer children than women who live in the countryside.[62]

Related to the total fertility rate is the *replacement rate*—the average number of live births needed to maintain stable population numbers. For most of human history, the replacement rate was quite high because, again, so many kids died before attaining adulthood. But when child mortality numbers plunged in recent years, the replacement rate did too. Today demographers put the global replacement rate at 2.1—that is, just over two children per woman, on average, in a given population.

> **NOTE:** A replacement rate of 2.1 is a good ballpark figure on a global scale, but it doesn't necessarily apply to every population. For example, in some countries—those plagued by poverty, famine, instability, or violence, or where boys are valued more highly than girls, skewing sex ratios at birth—the real replacement rate might be 3 or above. Still, 2.1 is a good rule of thumb.

MORTALITY RATE

In addition to tracking fertility rates, demographers also tabulate mortality rates. A population's mortality rate is typically presented as the number of deaths per one thousand individuals.

The mortality rate of any population is inextricably linked to its average life expectancy, which, in the last century or so, has soared. It's not that people never lived to old age before now; some did, though usually not past age sixty*ish*. But so many children died it distorted the average.

Thanks to advancements in medicine and sanitation, more children now survive, and more adults live to old age. Take Great Britain. In 1960 a male baby born in the United Kingdom could expect to live to the age of sixty-eight.[63] Now that number is seventy-nine, and for baby girls, it's eighty-two.[64]

IMMIGRATION

The third key input for population modeling is immigration—the number of people who migrate to a country.

When you boil it down, people emigrate from their homeland for two reasons. One is they're pushed. This happens when circumstances at home degenerate to the point that it's not safe for them to stay. Maybe there's political upheaval. Maybe there's a war. Maybe they're being persecuted for their religion or ethnicity. Or maybe some sort of natural disaster has occurred—an earthquake, a hurricane, a tsunami, a volcano eruption, a mudslide, a fire—that has destroyed their home or their town.

The other, more common, reason people move is they're pulled. They're drawn by better opportunities—a better job, a better life. Maybe their home country is impoverished, or their living conditions are poor. Maybe there are just too many people and not enough jobs to go around. Maybe they have career aspirations that require study at a respected university in another country.

> **Of the three inputs—fertility rate, mortality rate, and immigration—immigration is the hardest to forecast and therefore the most challenging to model.**

Of the three inputs—fertility rate, mortality rate, and immigration—immigration is the hardest to forecast and therefore the most challenging to model. This is because the circumstances that drive both push and pull migration are difficult to predict. On the push side, no one can say when a natural disaster might occur, or the political situation might deteriorate to a dangerous degree. And pull migration is difficult to detect because these movements tend to happen more slowly—over decades or even generations.

> **NOTE:** Countries whose fertility rate is below the replacement rate, including the United States, rely heavily on immigration to stabilize their population numbers.

OTHER IMPORTANT POPULATION METRICS

As far as inputs for population modeling go, fertility rate, death rate, and immigration are the "big three"—the factors on which demographers rely most heavily to forecast population changes. But they're lagging indicators. They tell us what's happened in the past, not what might happen in the future. So I like to consider leading metrics that might point to changes in these factors ahead of time, especially the fertility rate, which, as I mentioned, fluctuates the most.

I already talked about how variables such as child mortality, education, financial independence, views on work, and urbanization can affect fertility rates. But there are other variables worth examining:

- **CONTRACEPTION USE:** When contraception use goes up, fertility rates go down. That's just common sense.

- **MARRIAGE RATES:** According to researchers at Penn Wharton, a married woman is 3 percent more likely to have a child than an unmarried woman.[65] (Divorce rates provide some insight too because many couples divorce before having the number of children they might have preferred.)

- **MEDIAN AGE OF WOMEN AT MARRIAGE:** Those same Penn Wharton researchers observe that "[t]iming of marriage, and particularly whether a woman marries younger or older, has historically been a strong indicator of women's fertility patterns."[66]

- **AVERAGE AGE OF FIRST-TIME MOTHERS:** The younger a woman is when she delivers her first baby, the longer she has to deliver more (biologically speaking)—and by extension, the more children she is likely to have.[67] So because a woman's fertility declines to practically zero by the time she enters her midforties, if she doesn't start having kids until her midthirties, she won't have much time to have many more.

DELAYED MOTHERHOOD

As a whole, women in all industrialized countries now delay motherhood.[68] For example, between 1972 and 2022, the average age of first-time mothers in the United States rose from twenty-one to thirty years.[69] Why? Population economist Vegard Skirbekk poses a persuasive theory: "Status in modern societies requires time." That is, you must obtain higher education, climb the career ladder, buy a car and a house, identify a spouse, and attain financial security. All this, he says, "can take many years of reproductive life and imply postponed fertility."[70] Frankly, I think he's onto something.

- **THE NUMBER OF CHILDREN A COUPLE WANTS:** According to political economist Nicholas Eberstadt, "One of the most powerful predictors of fertility levels the world over—across countries, ethnicities, and time—turns out to be the number of children that women (also men) happen to want." Still, for various reasons, many of them financial in nature, many couples do not have as many children as they would like.[71]

- **THE STATE OF THE ECONOMY:** When the economy is good, birth rates often go up; when it's bad, they go down. As just one example, during the Great Recession between 2007 and 2010, birth rates in the United States dropped more than 7 percent.[72]

- **COST OF LIVING:** In some areas the cost of living (particularly housing) is prohibitively expensive. So some couples choose not to become parents because they feel they cannot afford to. For example, Canada's metropolitan areas, which have high housing costs, have lower fertility.[73]

- **AVAILABILITY AND COST OF CHILDCARE:** In the United States, the median annual cost of childcare in 2018 ranged from $4,801 to $15,417 ($5,357 to $17,171 in 2022 dollars), depending on the type of provider, the age of the child, and the county. That is *a lot* of money.

- **OTHER CHILD-RELATED EXPENSES:** Kids are *expensive*—and not just because of childcare costs. They eat. They need diapers. They need new clothes and shoes. There are school fees and music lessons and sports uniforms. Maybe they need braces. Maybe they need glasses. And college! Since 1970 the average cost of a public four-year college—including tuition, room, and board—has ballooned from $1,238 per year ($9,338 in 2023 dollars) to $21,337 today,[74] while the cost of private college has inflated from $2,754 ($20,772 in 2023 dollars) to $46,313.[75] The sheer cost associated with raising children puts off many prospective parents from conceiving or causes them to have fewer kids than they would like.

- **INCOME:** In general, lower-income women have more children than higher-income women. But recently, that trend has begun to reverse, at least in the United States. Here, women with high incomes may feel more inclined to have children because they know they can afford them.[76] (Then again, those same women might have a higher income because they are career oriented, meaning they might prefer *not* to have more children.)

NOTE: Some social scientists worry that "poorer families may be poor because they have chosen to invest their money in children, and richer families may be rich because they have not," says Jonathan V. Last in *What to Expect When No One's Expecting.*[77]

- **DEBT:** There's ample evidence that high debt—student debt in particular (at least in the United States)—deters people from starting families.[78]

- **VIEWS ON PARENTING:** Anyone who has had kids in the past thirty years knows that parenting has become an all-consuming endeavor. Indeed, today's working moms spend almost as much time with their kids as stay-at-home moms did in 1965.[79] These "changing norms regarding the intensity of parenting might change prospective parents' decisions on how many children to have or whether to have children at all," say economists Melissa S. Kearney and Phillip B. Levine of the Aspen Institute.[80]

- **IMPORTANCE OF LEISURE TIME:** The consuming nature of parenthood means parents have less leisure time. (There are, after all, only twenty-four hours in a day!) A total of 36 percent of young adults who responded to a 2018 survey by the *New York Times* cited "want leisure time" as one reason they don't plan to have kids.[81]

- **VIEWS ON CLIMATE CHANGE:** Most young people feel pretty gloomy about climate change, so much so that some of them have decided to have fewer kids (or none at all). (I talk more about this in Chapter 5.)

- **EMPLOYMENT RATES AMONG YOUNG MEN:** Increased access to education and income has caused women in some societies to become more selective. "Even in the world's most gender-egalitarian countries, women tend to prefer men with relatively high income and education," says Skirbekk.[82] That usually means men must be employed to be considered "suitable."

- **ACCEPTANCE OF LGBTQ+ RIGHTS:** Before societies began to acknowledge the rights of LGBTQ+ people, many of them "often unhappily made do with heterosexual life," says Last—and that included having children with their spouse. Of course, LGBTQ+ people still have children, usually through adoption or surrogacy, but not nearly as many as straight couples.[83]

- **RELIGIOUS OBSERVANCE:** Religious people tend to have higher fertility rates. (This is true even of people who aren't religious but whose parents are.) Adam Carrington at Law &

Liberty suggests that this may be because religion "recognizes the special importance of making and raising children."[84]

> **NOTE:** Identifying leading metrics for mortality rates and immigration can be a bit more difficult, as these might be tied to specific unpredictable events—for example, the emergence of a deadly pathogen or the development of a cure for cancer on the mortality side or a natural disaster or political upheaval on the immigration front. So demographers typically rely more on historical data to calculate these two factors.

WHO GENERATES POPULATION FORECASTS?

Most countries track their own population numbers, usually by way of a census. Various international organizations then gather and synthesize this information to monitor the global population and generate forecasts.

The most prominent of these organizations is the United Nations Department of Economic and Social Affairs Population Division (UNPD). Established in 1946, the UNPD (in its own words) "conducts demographic research, supports intergovernmental processes at the United Nations in the area of population and development, and assists countries in developing their capacity to produce and analyse population data and information."[85] As part of that charter, the division "prepares population estimates and projections as well as estimates of the international migrant stock for all countries in the world on a regular basis."[86] Every few years the UNPD releases these estimates and projections in a report called *World Population Prospects*.

When modeling population, the UNPD runs thousands of statistical simulations to identify what it calls the *medium variant*. This variant, says the UNPD, "is derived by aggregating the 'best guess' projections for individual countries and areas." An implicit assumption of the medium variant is that "the pace and patterns of change in these variables will be similar in the future to what they have been in the past seventy years." This variant also assumes "a slight increase in the level of fertility … for countries where women are having, on average, fewer than two births over a lifetime."[87]

> **NOTE:** These assumptions are important, and I'll come back to them in chapter 4.

From this medium variant, the UNPD generates additional variants, including the following:

- **HIGH VARIANT:** This variant assumes that the fertility rate for each population will be 0.5 births higher than with the medium variant. So for example, if the medium variant assumes that the fertility rate for a particular population will be 1.8, the high variant assumes it will be 2.3.

- **LOW VARIANT:** This variant assumes that each population's fertility rate will be 0.5 births *lower* than the medium variant—in this example, 1.3 instead of 1.8.

Table 2.1 shows the UNPD's population projections for the high, low, and medium variants in 2050 and 2100, as well as where and when the global population will peak. Figure 2.2 offers a visual representation.

Table 2.1. UNPD population projections: Low, medium, and high variants (2050 and 2100)[88]

VARIANT	2050 POPULATION (IN BILLIONS)	2100 POPULATION (IN BILLIONS)	PEAK (IN BILLIONS) /YEAR
Low	8.3	7.043	8.939/2053
Medium	9.7	10.349	10.431/2086
High	10.9	14.8	*

*In the high variant, population is not projected to peak until after 2100.

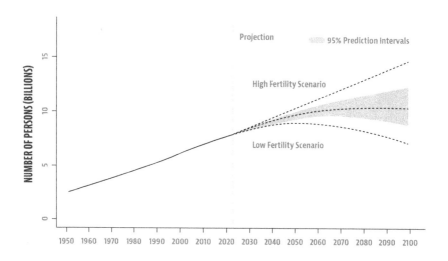

Figure 2.2. UNPD population forecasts (high, medium, and low variants) (Source: United Nations Department of Economic and Social Affairs Population Division)

NOTE: The widening band in figure 2.2 that emerges from the medium variant as it moves rightward reflects the increasing uncertainty that naturally arises the farther out one tries to predict.

The UNPD generates other variants too. The most recent report, published in 2022, contained ten variants in all. Three of these variants were the aforementioned low, medium, and high variants. Six of the variants were similar to these three but used different fertility, mortality, and immigration figures. But one variant included a newer input called *momentum*, introduced in 2017. I'll talk more about the momentum input in chapter 4.

Of all these variants, the UNPD contends that the medium variant "can be interpreted as the most likely future trend."[89] I'm not so sure that's right—and neither are some other organizations that predict population trends.

One of these organizations is the Wittgenstein Centre for Demography and Global Human Capital, a collaboration between the Austrian Academy of Sciences (ÖAW), the International Institute for Applied Systems Analysis (IIASA), and the University of Vienna. Founded in 2011, the Wittgenstein Centre, or WC-IIASA, analyzes population dynamics and human capital. It contends that the global population won't peak at 10.431 billion in 2086, as indicated by the UNPD's medium variant. Rather, it will crest at 9.8 billion in 2070. And in 2100, the global population won't be 10.349 billion; it will be 9.5 billion.[90]

Another is IHME at the University of Washington School of Medicine. Founded in 2007 with the support of the Bill & Melinda Gates Foundation, the IHME's mission is to deliver timely, relevant, and scientifically valid evidence to improve health policy and practice. In 2017 IMHE researchers took a fresh look at the approach used by the UNPD and other organizations to forecast regional, national, and global populations and modified it to account for various drivers of changes in fertility and mortality—things such as education and use of contraceptives. Their forecast, published in the *Lancet* in 2020, predicts that the global population will apex at 9.6 billion in 2064 and taper to 8.8 billion by 2100.[91] Again, this is well below the UNPD's medium variant.

Which scenario is right? I have my theories, and I'll talk about them in chapter 4. First, though, I'll get into what steps were taken by governments around the world to defuse the Malthusian nightmare described in chapter 1, how effective they were, and how our world changed as a result.

CHAPTER 3

DEFUSING THE POPULATION BOMB

The world is now full ... And the regulation of population has become one of the most essential of international problems.

—WILLIAM VOGT, AUTHOR OF *ROAD TO SURVIVAL*

D uring the twentieth century, Malthusian fever gripped much of the developed world. The prevailing view in boardrooms, drawing rooms, government agencies, and on the ground was that an ever-growing population put everyone in danger. Even earth itself was at risk.

Dr. Paul Ehrlich of *The Population Bomb* fame identified two solutions to what he called the "population problem." The first was the "birth rate solution," which involved lowering the birth rate to zero. The second was the "death rate solution," in which "ways to raise the death rate—war, famine, pestilence—find us."[92] Ehrlich believed

49

this second "solution" was inescapable without immediate and drastic action to limit our population—and even that likely would not be enough.

Galvanized by a growing sense of urgency, private organizations and government agencies across the developed world assembled a variety of programs to avert what they saw as a crisis. Some of these were agricultural programs, whose purpose was to identify new ways to increase food production to stave off famine. Others were programs designed to drive down birth rates, particularly in less-developed countries (LDCs). This chapter explores some of these programs—who initiated them, what they were, and whether they were effective.

> **Galvanized by a growing sense of urgency, private organizations and government agencies across the developed world assembled a variety of programs to avert what they saw as a crisis.**

AGRICULTURE: THE GREEN REVOLUTION

Long before Ehrlich sounded the alarm on population growth in 1968—indeed, even before Henry Fairfield Osborn Jr. and William Vogt wrote their screeds on the topic in 1948—efforts were underway to devise new farming techniques to boost crop yields. One of these was the Cooperative Wheat Research Production Program in Mexico, a joint venture between the Mexican government and the Rockefeller Foundation in New York, launched in 1943. The purpose of this program was to research soil development, maize and wheat production, and plant pathology (that is, plant diseases) to avert food shortages.

Among the scientists working on this program was an American named Norman Borlaug. Borlaug was born and raised on his family's 106-acre plot near Cresco, Iowa. Like most farm kids, he had worked the land starting from a young age. But Borlaug did more than just work the land: he *wondered* about it. "Growing things fascinated him from his childhood," said his sister, Palma. "He always had a feeling for plants, a passionate desire to know how they grew."[93]

Borlaug earned a bachelor's degree in forestry at the University of Minnesota in 1937, a master's degree in plant pathology and genetics in 1940, and a PhD in those same subjects in 1942. His work initially involved crossbreeding strains of wheat to develop hybrid cultivars that resisted disease and flourished even in harsh climates.

In Mexico, Borlaug shifted his focus to developing an entirely new type of cultivar—a short-stemmed ("dwarf") wheat plant that tolerated larger quantities of fertilizer, produced more edible kernels, and yielded dramatically larger crops *without* consuming more land. In this, Borlaug succeeded, and boy, was it a game changer. Between 1944 and 1970, Mexican wheat yields multiplied by a factor of four, from 750 kilograms per hectare to roughly 3,000.[94]

> **NOTE:** Borlaug's work represents an early foray into the field of genetically modified organisms (GMOs). While some find GMOs controversial, they've undeniably played an enormous role in combating hunger all over the world.

Other countries took note, especially those with looming food shortages of their own. In 1963 Borlaug fielded requests from the Indian and Pakistani governments for assistance in increasing their wheat yields. Again with the support of the Rockefeller Foundation, this time in collaboration with the Food and Agricultural Organization of the UN, Borlaug supplied both countries with Mexican dwarf varieties for wide-scale testing. The results were positive. In India wheat production grew from 12 million metric tons in 1965 to more than 20 million in 1970.[95]

The success of Borlaug's Mexican dwarf wheat variants inspired scientists to experiment with other grains to develop similarly hardy and bountiful strains that required less land to grow. Through decades of work and close collaboration, these scientists developed high-yield varieties of rice, sorghum millet, maize, cassava, and beans. They even designed some crops to withstand severe or unusual environmental conditions, such as flood-resistant, drought-proof, and salt-tolerant varieties of rice.

Collectively, these advancements, combined with other agricultural developments such as increased mechanization, became known as the *green revolution*. Its impact cannot be overstated. Thanks to the green revolution, farmers in 2021 produced more than 240 percent more grains than in 1961, improved their crop yields by more than 200 percent, and yet consumed just over 13 percent more land.[96] Without the green revolution, says agricultural ecologist Gordon Conway, "the numbers of poor and hungry today would be far greater."[97] Indeed, some experts claim that the green revolution spared as many as a billion people worldwide from starvation and death.

NOTE: The green revolution made manifest a theory famously espoused by twentieth-century Danish economist Esther Boserup. Boserup, an early cornucopian, believed that crises (such as an impending famine) inspire major innovation, so food production would naturally increase to meet growing population levels.

The green revolution spurred other improvements too. Farmers in undeveloped areas who planted these new varietals to increase their yields also increased their incomes. At the same time, food prices went down. As a result everyone had more money to spend on other goods and services, which in turn stimulated the broader rural economy and generated additional employment and income. This scenario played out in Asia, where real capital incomes—for everyone, not just farmers—almost doubled between 1970 and 1995.[98]

> **NOTE:** Because of the increased use of machines in farming, fewer people were needed to work the land. In this way the green revolution also fueled urbanization.

As successful as the green revolution was, it had its problems, particularly from an environmental perspective. The high-yield crops that epitomize the green revolution require significant amounts of fertilizer and pesticide. This, says science writer Peter Hazell, has "polluted waterways, poisoned agricultural workers, affected the health of the general population, and killed beneficial insects and other wildlife."[99] High-yield crops also consume much more water, so much so that "water, rather than land, is the new constraint on food production in much of the world today," observes Fred Pearce in *The Coming Population Crash*.[100] Finally, the type of farming heralded by the green revolution can pollute the air, damage the soil, choke out indigenous flora, and drive down biodiversity among wild plants.

Critics of the green revolution also claim it left small farmers behind. "Small farmers did lag behind large farmers in adopting Green Revolution technologies," says Hazell. But he says, "Many of them eventually did so." Some small farmers "actually ended up gaining proportionally more income than larger farmers."[101] But even if they didn't, they likely benefited, at least to some extent, from the rising rural economy that resulted from the green revolution.

In 1970, Borlaug, often called the "Father of the Green Revolution," won the Nobel Peace Prize. During his acceptance speech, Borlaug observed, "Some critics have said that the green revolution has created more problems than it has solved. This I cannot accept, for I believe it is far better for mankind to be struggling with new problems caused by abundance rather than with the old problem of famine."[102]

Fortunately, a new generation of scientists has joined in this struggle: developing new and sustainable farming practices to address environmental concerns, cultivating and preserving endangered plant species to save them from extinction, inventing new tools to stave off plant diseases, and distributing the world's bounty to the areas that need it the most, all while using less and less arable land.

CURBING REPRODUCTION

Norman Borlaug believed wholeheartedly in the promise of the green revolution. But he thought it was only one piece of the puzzle. During that same 1970 Nobel Peace Prize acceptance speech, Borlaug warned, "The frightening power of human reproduction must also be curbed; otherwise, the success of the green revolution will be ephemeral only."[103] As it happened, efforts to curb human reproduction were already underway.

CONTRACEPTION AND FAMILY PLANNING

On an individual level, women have engaged in practices to prevent or terminate pregnancies for thousands of years. Ancient Greek, Roman,

Egyptian, and Arabic literature mention a variety of contraceptives, or birth control, "from crocodile-dung pessaries to barriers and postcoital sponges and potions like honey and pepper," says Pearce. In fact, "Many herbs used then are now known to contain chemicals that act as contraceptives, induce menstruation, or are outright abortifacients."[104]

NOTE: An early reference to male contraception appears around 3000 BCE in a Greek myth about King Minos of Knossos. According to this myth, the king wore a goat's bladder as a condom to protect his mistresses from serpents and scorpions in his semen.[105]

Women employed these and other methods, including abortion, to control their fertility until the Middle Ages. But in the aftermath of the Black Death in the mid-1300s, in which populations plunged, the Catholic Church prohibited all practices intended to prevent pregnancy. So knowledge of these ancient methods was lost or morphed into old wives' tales, at least in Europe. The Catholic Church has maintained this position on contraceptives for centuries. Even today its official stance on the matter is that birth control is intrinsically evil.

During the 1800s some countries declared birth control illegal. For example, in 1873 the United States passed the Comstock Law— the first of many federal and local "decency" laws that deemed birth control "obscene," criminalized its use, and prohibited anyone, even doctors, from disseminating information about it.

The criminalization of contraception posed a serious problem. Advances in medicine and sanitation meant more children survived to adulthood. So it was no longer necessary to have several children simply to ensure that at least some of them might survive. And the Industrial Revolution drew many families from farms to cities or towns, where having more children presented a variety of challenges. Criminalizing contraception made it impossible for women to adapt their fertility to their changed circumstances, so they often bore far more children than they could manage.

MARGARET SANGER AND THE PUSH FOR LEGAL CONTRACEPTION

In the early 1900s, a nurse in the slums of New York City named Margaret Sanger treated many such women. She witnessed their suffering, and sometimes their death, due to complications during pregnancy and birth. She also noted the crushing poverty they endured because of the number of children they bore.

To stop this senseless misery, Sanger began publishing pamphlets about contraception in 1914. Two years later she founded the nation's first birth control clinic. For this, Sanger was arrested, tried, and convicted under the Comstock Law and served thirty days in jail. Sanger appealed her conviction, and although she lost her case, she did persuade the court to grant doctors the right to prescribe contraceptives for medical reasons.

Over the next three decades, Sanger became the face and voice of the American birth control movement. She established several women's clinics nationwide and founded numerous organizations—one of which eventually evolved into the Planned Parenthood Federation of America—to promote contraception and to lobby for its full legalization.

All this was great. But what Sanger *really* wanted was to develop what she called a "magic tablet"—a 100 percent effective oral contraceptive that would empower women to control whether they fell pregnant.

In 1951 Sanger met an experimental biologist named Gregory Goodwin Pincus. Once a respected Harvard professor, Pincus had been cast out of academia in the late 1930s for conducting controversial research involving in vitro fertilization. By the time Pincus met Sanger, he was at best a fringe figure. Still, Sanger asked Pincus if he thought he could develop a birth control pill. Pincus answered that yes, he thought he could.

Finding funding for this project was no easy task. Several federal and local laws still prohibited not only the use of contraceptives (unless prescribed by a doctor for medical purposes) but also scientific research involving birth control. So exactly zero pharmaceutical companies were willing to invest in the development of Sanger's "magic tablet." However, Sanger was acquainted with a wealthy heiress named Katharine Dexter McCormick who *was* willing. All told, McCormick would spend more than $2 million of her own money to bankroll Sanger's project.

In 1955 Pincus publicly announced the successful development of an oral contraceptive, which became known as simply *the pill*. His announcement prompted women across America to demand immediate access to this new form of contraception. It also compelled the G.D. Searle pharmaceutical company to manufacture the pill, which they called *Enovid*, and to apply to the FDA for approval. In 1957 the FDA approved Enovid not for birth control—that wouldn't happen until 1960—but for "menstrual disorders." Still, the unrestricted use of contraceptives remained illegal until 1965 for married couples and until 1972 for unmarried people.

MARGARET SANGER'S COMPLICATED LEGACY

Margaret Sanger's contributions to women's health and autonomy cannot be denied. Indeed, all hormonal contraception available today descends from Sanger's "magic tablet." Her legacy is complicated, however, by her alliance with eugenicists.

Sanger believed the eugenics movement complemented her efforts to promote the use of contraception, noting in 1920 that "birth control is nothing more or less than the facilitation of the process of weeding out the unfit [and] of preventing the birth of defectives."[106] Sanger also supported the sterilization of the "unfit" and endorsed a 1927 Supreme Court decision that confirmed the constitutionality of this practice in the United States.

These are, of course, deplorable views. But they were shared among many erudite and respected people of the day, including Theodore Roosevelt, Alexander Graham Bell, Helen Keller, Winston Churchill, W. E. B. Du Bois, Clarence Darrow, George Bernard Shaw, and John D. Rockefeller Jr. Ultimately, "Margaret Sanger tried to co-opt eugenics in a bid for respectability," her grandson, Alexander Sanger, has said. "It failed miserably and the damage continues to this day."[107]

JOHN D. ROCKEFELLER III AND THE POPULATION COUNCIL

Escalating concerns about population growth in LDCs such as China, India, and other (it should be said, primarily non-white) states in the aftermath of World War II also caused a shift in attitudes about contraception. Indeed, even as birth control remained illegal in the United States, private American organizations and, later, the US government distributed contraceptives and provided other family planning services to LDCs around the world.

A key figure in this effort was John D. Rockefeller III. In 1952, after reading apocalyptic books such as those by Henry Fairfield Osborn Jr. and William Vogt, Rockefeller formed an organization called the Population Council. With significant funding from the Rockefeller Brothers Fund (not to be confused with the Rockefeller Foundation), the Population Council, in its own words, "approached population through basic medical research, effective and affordable contraceptives, educational outreach, technical assistance, professional training, and long-term planning studies."[108] It would become, says Pearce, "the most influential clearinghouse for ideas and policies for family planning and population control."[109]

NOTE: The Population Council became such a fixture in American Society it even partnered with Disney to produce an animated short called *Family Planning*, starring Donald Duck, in 1967.

The Population Council established research centers and family planning clinics in several countries around the world. But Rockefeller believed the US federal government could do even more. As it happened, a government report issued in 1959 agreed with him. This report—called the Draper Report, after the leader of the committee that issued it, William H. Draper Jr.—found that population growth in LDCs canceled needed economic gains and concluded that the US government should extend aid to these countries for family planning and fertility control. However, President Dwight D. Eisenhower disagreed, noting, "I cannot imagine anything more emphatically a subject that is not a proper political or governmental activity or function or responsibility ... [than] this problem of birth control."[110]

President John F. Kennedy, who took office in 1960, was similarly disinclined to pursue efforts to influence fertility abroad. But a publicity campaign by various Rockefeller associates persuaded members of Congress to pass the Foreign Assistance Act of 1961, which included noncoercive population control efforts as one criterion (among many) for determining which countries should receive foreign aid of any kind, which Kennedy signed into law.

Initially, the purpose of these family planning programs was to educate people in LDCs on preventing pregnancies, *not* to distribute contraception.

In 1965 American officials began earmarking funds for family planning programs in LDCs to limit population growth, organized by a new bureau within the US State Department: the Agency for International Development (then called AID and now referred to as USAID). By the end of that decade, the United States had expanded these programs around the world at a cost of some $100 million a year (roughly $800 million in today's dollars).[111] And by 1973, the same year abortion became legal in the United States, the importance of population control had become so entrenched among lawmakers that they amended the Foreign Assistance Act to list population planning as one of five basic human needs (the others being food and nutrition, health, education, and human resources development).

Initially, the purpose of these family planning programs was to educate people in LDCs on preventing pregnancies, *not* to distribute contraception. In fact, the distribution of contraception by USAID was explicitly banned. In 1967, however, this ban was lifted, and since then USAID has distributed billions of condoms and oral contraceptives and millions of IUDs, implants, and injectables. This has empowered women in some of the least-developed areas on earth to gain control of their fertility, freeing them to seek education, obtain meaningful work, improve their standard of living, and increase their autonomy.

> **NOTE:** USAID was just one organization that funded efforts to curb population. Others included the World Bank, UNFPA, the Ford Foundation, and the Swedish International Development Authority.

Family planning programs were important. But the confidential Kissinger Report, distributed to government officials in 1974, recognized that other steps could help curb population by "creating conditions conducive to fertility decline." Specifically, the report suggested prioritizing "selective development policies in sectors offering the greatest promise of increased motivation for smaller family size." These policies included

> providing minimal levels of education, especially for women; reducing infant mortality, including through simple low-cost health care networks; expanding wage employment, especially for women; developing alternatives to children as a source of old age security; increasing income of the poorest, especially in rural areas, including providing privately owned

farms; [and] education of new generations on the desirability of smaller families.[112]

COERCIVE GOVERNMENT INTERVENTIONS

Participation in family planning programs such as those supported by USAID was generally voluntary. But many countries initiated coercive measures to slow population growth and, in some cases, cull "unfit" groups. These measures included forced sterilization, typically tubal ligation for women and vasectomies for men, and laws to limit the number of children allowed per couple.

FORCED STERILIZATION

Some nations practiced forced or involuntary sterilization to control the size of their population or to reduce the proliferation of the "unfit." One obvious example is Nazi Germany, which sterilized roughly half a million people during the 1930s and 1940s. Other examples include Japan, which sterilized more than twenty-five thousand people between 1948 and 1996 (and even today forces transgender people to be sterilized if they elect to switch genders), and Czechoslovakia, which legalized the involuntary sterilization of Roma women in 1971 after *illegally* sterilizing them starting in 1966 (and perhaps even before that).

In the United States, even as US law prohibited the use of contraceptives, it allowed for the compulsory sterilization of certain inhabitants. "Between the first and second world wars, some sixty thousand imbeciles, epileptics, and 'feebleminded' persons were compulsorily sterilized in the United States," says Pearce.[113] American officials also sterilized an estimated one-third of all Puerto Rican women of childbearing age between 1936 and 1968.[114] And during the second half of the twentieth century, both the United States and Canada sterilized substantial numbers of indigenous women.[115]

As extensive as these sterilization operations were, one in India was even more so. It began after Prime Minister Indira Gandhi declared a national emergency in 1975, suspended the country's constitution and further elections, and jailed many of her opponents. Although Prime Minister Gandhi cited "internal disturbance" as the reason for these maneuvers, historians say her *real* motive was to retain power after being convicted of electoral malpractice. To secure her position, Gandhi needed considerable foreign aid, which was contingent upon the implementation of population control programs. So in 1976 and 1977, a period called the Emergency, Gandhi and her son Sanjay oversaw a gruesome campaign to forcibly sterilize nearly eleven million people, most of them men.[116] In 1977, facing mass protests and threats of armed revolt, Gandhi rescinded the Emergency and terminated India's compulsory sterilization operation. But the Indian government still pays Indians, mostly impoverished women, to be sterilized.

BIRTH LIMITS

Imposing limits on birth was another approach to reducing population. In some countries, such as South Korea, limiting births was encouraged but not mandatory; other countries, such as Singapore, Myanmar, and Vietnam, enacted laws with harsh penalties to prevent couples from bearing more than a certain number of children. (These laws have since been rescinded.)

Then there was China.

During the Communist reign of Chairman Mao Zedong, which lasted from 1949 to 1976, the Chinese population spiked from 540 million to 930 million.[117] This was by design. Chairman Mao believed, "The more people, the stronger we are."[118] Another government official, Hu Yaobang, put it this way: "The force of 600 million liberated people is tens of thousands of times stronger than a nuclear explosion."[119] But this force was also, writes Laura Fitzpatrick at *Time*, "nearly as destructive."[120] By 1962 a massive famine had claimed the lives of as many as 45 million Chinese people.[121]

Spooked by this scarcity, Communist officials launched a propaganda campaign to stem population growth, but Mao's Cultural Revolution, launched in 1966, quickly extinguished it. Five years, though, the Chinese government renewed the campaign, and this time it stuck.

As part of this campaign, the Chinese government popularized a new slogan, "Wan, Xi, Shao" ("Late, Long, and Few"), to urge couples to marry later (in their mid- to late twenties), to wait longer for their first baby and at least three years between babies, and to have fewer babies (two in cities and three in rural areas). The government also provided free contraceptives and increased access to abortions and sterilization services.[122]

The "Wan, Xi, Shao" campaign reduced fertility rates, from 5.43 in 1971 to 2.92 in 1979.[123] But because of population momentum, China's population continued to climb, from 843 million in 1971 to 968 million in 1979.[124] (I'll explain what population momentum is in chapter 4.)

To Deng Xiaoping, who assumed control of the Communist party after Mao's death in 1976, this was extremely concerning. He believed that unless China reduced its birth rate, "We will not be able to develop our economy and raise the living standards of our people."[125] In 1980, with Deng's support, the Chinese government introduced a controversial new policy that limited couples to just one child.

> **NOTE:** The policy allowed couples in rural areas to have a second baby, five years after the birth of their first. Couples in urban areas, however, were granted no such exception.

Enforcement of the one-child policy was nothing short of draconian. "Heads were counted, abortions enforced, and even menstrual cycles monitored,"[126] says Pearce. Those who violated the policy faced punishments that ranged from "heavy fines to confiscation of belongings to dismissal from work," says author Jonathan V. Last in *What to Expect When No One's Expecting.*[127]

Because Chinese culture placed a higher value on boys than girls, government officials encouraged women to abort female babies in utero or to kill them after they were born so they could try again for a boy. When women carried "illegal" babies to term, officials routinely seized them and placed them up for adoption by foreign couples. More than 100,000 Chinese infants, overwhelmingly girls, were adopted abroad.[128] If a couple was lucky enough to keep an "illegal" baby, they were charged exorbitant fees, and their child was denied standing to study, work, marry, or have children of their own.

> **NOTE:** Because so many female infants were aborted, killed, or adopted abroad, there are at least 30 million more Chinese men than there are Chinese women. This type of skewed ratio poses a host of problems and, says Last, "has often preceded intense violence and instability."[129]

I'll say one thing for the one-child policy: it was effective. Chinese officials estimate that the policy prevented some 400 million births.[130]

Ultimately, though, it worked a little *too* well. China's fertility rate dropped from 2.75 in 1979 (the year before the introduction of the one-child policy) to 1.18 in 2022—well below the replacement rate.[131] The UNPD projects that between 2022 and 2050, the country's total population will fall by nearly 120 million people.[132] That's its medium-variant projection. If the low-variant projection is correct, China's population will fall even more.

This drop has already begun and much earlier than anticipated. In 2019 demographers at the US Census Bureau and the UN predicted that China's population would begin dropping in the early 2030s. But according to Chinese officials, the country shed 850,000 people in 2022.[133]

Confronted with this immutable math, the Chinese government replaced its one-child policy with a two-child policy in 2016. This did result in a bump in the fertility rate, but just a small one, and it didn't last. So in May 2021, the government replaced its two-child policy with a three-child policy, and in 2023 one Chinese province removed birth limits altogether. Chinese officials have even begun designing and implementing policies to *encourage* people to have kids, including expanding the national health insurance system to cover in vitro fertilization.[134] Think about that: in a span of just seven years, the Chinese government has gone from dramatically limiting childbirth to loosening restrictions, to encouraging birth, to actually assisting couples in getting pregnant. It's astonishing!

Still, few Chinese couples have shown much interest in having more (or any) children. "In 2022, China had only about half as many births as just six years earlier (9.6 million vs. 17.9 million)," says political economist Nicholas Eberstadt.[135] Why? Lots of reasons: Kids are expensive, having a kid could prevent women from pursuing a fulfilling career, and many couples are busy caring for their aging parents, to name a few. Unless those (and other) problems get solved, Chinese couples are unlikely to change their reproductive habits.

CRISIS AVERTED

It's tempting today to mock the Malthusians of the midtwentieth century because few (if any) of their predictions came true. Ecological collapse did not trigger nuclear war; hundreds of millions of people did not starve during the 1970s; society did not break down.

In fact, in many respects, the state of the world is objectively better than ever. Between 1950 and 2020, the global average income rose 307 percent, from $4,158 to $16,904—an increase that was particularly pronounced in China (1,936 percent) and India (690 percent).[136] As Marian Tupy and Gale Pooley write in *Superabundance*, "The growth of the human population from roughly 1 billion in 1800 to 7.8 billion in 2020 has not been accompanied by a lowering of living standards but by an explosion in material abundance."[137]

Meanwhile, between 1960 and 2017, the average global life expectancy grew from 52.6 years to 72.4 years (37.6 percent). Again, China and India saw the most significant gains, from 43.7 years to 76.4 years (75 percent) in China and from 41.2 years to 68.8 years (67 percent) in India.[138] Contributing to this positive trend was the global infant mortality rate, which plummeted from 64.7 to 28.9 (55 percent) during roughly the same period.[139]

That's not all. Between 1961 and 2017, the global average food supply per person rose from 2,115 calories to 2,917 calories (38 percent), well over the United States Department of Agriculture's recommended daily amount, thanks in no small part to Norman Borlaug and the green revolution.[140] Tupy and Pooley say, "Today, obesity tends to be a bigger problem than starvation in many parts of the world, and famines have disappeared outside of active war zones."[141]

Still, the events predicted by modern Malthusians *might* have transpired if private organizations and government agencies hadn't launched various initiatives to avert what they believed was a looming crisis. That being said, one must acknowledge that although (most of) these initiatives were well intentioned and that the people who championed and administered them believed they were doing the right thing, many of them were racist in nature and often had negative consequences. But in the end, these programs achieved their objective: they defused the population bomb.

CHAPTER 4

THE FALLACY OF OVERPOPULATION

These are probably the lowest rates of fertility
in nonsuicidal populations in history. The only
time like it was after the First World War, when a
generation of young men died on the battlefield.

—FRED PEARCE, AUTHOR OF
THE COMING POPULATION CRASH

Since the emergence of Malthusian thought at the turn of the nineteenth century, the overwhelming consensus has been that our ever-growing population poses an existential threat to people and our planet. This belief spurred private organizations and government agencies to institute programs to slash birth rates both at home and abroad during the twentieth century. Even today pretty much everyone seems to believe the world is experiencing an overpopulation epidemic!

Is this really true? I don't think so. I believe it's much more likely that our world population will crest sooner than later and that when it does, it will quickly fall ... fast and forever. In this chapter, I'll prove my case.

UN POPULATION PROJECTIONS: A BRIEF REVIEW

Before I prove why we are more likely to face underpopulation than overpopulation, let's briefly review how the UNPD calculates population forecasts.

Every few years the UNPD releases a report, called *World Population Prospects*, which contains several population forecasts, or *variants*. The most recent version of this report as of this writing, issued in 2022, contains ten such variants. Nine of these use differing values for three main inputs: fertility rate, mortality rate, and immigration. The tenth variant adds a new input, called *momentum*, which I'll talk about in the next section.

Of these ten variants, the UNPD focuses primarily on three: a medium variant, a high variant (which assumes the fertility rate will be 0.5 births higher than the medium variant), and a low variant (which assumes the fertility rate will be 0.5 births lower). Table 4.1 shows the UNPD's 2022 population projections for the high, low, and medium variants. (If you're experiencing déjà vu, it's because you saw this same table in chapter 2.)

Table 4.1. UN population projections: low, medium, and high variants (2050 and 2100)[142]

SCENARIO	2050 POPULATION (IN BILLIONS)	2100 POPULATION (IN BILLIONS)	PEAK (IN BILLIONS) /YEAR
Low	8.3	7.043	8.939/2053
Medium	9.7	10.349	10.431/2086
High	10.9	14.8	*

*With the high variant, population is not projected to peak until after 2100.

Of these three scenarios, UNPD demographers believe the medium scenario, in which the population balloons to 10.431 billion people in 2086 and then begins to contract, will most likely prove correct. Why? Because that's what's happened in the past. Of all the variants, the middle one has consistently yielded the most accurate predictions. I'm not saying it's spot-on. It's not. But considering all the moving pieces involved, it comes pretty darned close.

It's eminently rational to assume the medium scenario will continue this winning streak—lots of demographers do. But for all kinds of reasons, which I'll get into next, I'm not so sure.

THE INACCURATE NATURE OF LONG-TERM PREDICTIONS

Predicting population numbers and fertility rates in the short term—say, the next twenty to thirty years—isn't too hard. You simply extrapolate birth, death, and migration rates from recent trends. Will you be 100 percent on the nose? No. But barring some major upheaval (COVID-19 comes to mind), you'll probably be relatively close.

Making these types of predictions over the long term, several decades or more, is another story. "Projections diverge and become less reliable," says Spencer Bokat-Lindell in the *New York Times*, "in part because technological and environmental shocks that could cause demographic swings are impossible to predict."[143] These might include unexpected events such as "the outbreak of war, the impact of ... epidemics, natural disaster such as flood, cyclones and famine, economic boom, and the urgency of skill migration, etc.," say demographers Hafiz Khan and Wolfgang Lutz.[144] However, most models, including those generated by the UNPD, bake in some element of uncertainty to account for these types of events.

FALSE ASSUMPTIONS

All projections rely on a certain set of assumptions, and projections published by the UNPD are no exception. One of these assumptions I've already mentioned: because the medium scenario has been the most accurate in the past, it will be the most accurate in the future. The UNPD assumes this because, in its words, "the pace and patterns of change in [fertility, mortality, and immigration rates] will be similar in the future to what they have been in the past seventy years."[145] Is this really true? How do they know this? Sure, past is *usually* prologue—but not always!

Another assumption, stated by UNPD director John Wilmoth, is this: "We imagine that countries that currently have higher levels of fertility and lower levels of life expectancy will make progress in the future in a similar manner, at a similar speed, to what was experienced by countries in the past."[146] In other words the UN assumes that rates of fertility decline and increases in life expectancy will be the same from country to country or region to region. Again, is this really true? And again, how do they know?

Then there's this: with the medium variant, the UNPD relies on time as the only determinant for future trends in fertility and mortality. This does not "allow for alternative scenarios linked to policies or other drivers of fertility and mortality," say demographers at IHME.[147]

The UNPD also does not consider the effects of aging populations. Common sense would dictate that a population made up of mostly older women would produce a different number of children than a population made up of mostly younger women, yet this does not factor into the UNPD's forecasts.

Finally, here's an assumption I find particularly confusing: that countries with low fertility rates will somehow rebound to replacement rates. "The UN assumes this for countries where fertility has been in an uninterrupted decline for more than a half a century," says Jonathan V. Last in *What to Expect When No One's Expecting*.[148]

Here's how the UNPD explains this position:

> In several low-fertility countries, recent surveys have indicated that many women are having fewer children than they would like [because] women face multiple obstacles to achieving their desired family size—demands of higher education, high costs of childcare, challenges to work-family balance, unequal division of household tasks between partners, care responsibilities for ageing parents and biological limits to the reproductive life span.[149]

So they say, "Addressing these constraints will help to ensure that all individuals will have the opportunity and means to achieve family sizes that they desire."[150] But what evidence does the UNPD have that these constraints will be addressed?

One more thing: I said earlier that in recent years, the UNPD has begun generating a *momentum* scenario. This scenario shows the impact of a population's age structure on long-term population change. Simply put, says the UNPD, "a youthful population with constant levels of mortality and a net migration of zero continues to grow even when fertility remains constant at the replacement level."[151]

So "a relatively youthful age structure promotes a more rapid growth, because the births being produced by the relatively large number of women of reproductive age outnumber the deaths occurring in the total population, even if the fertility of the average woman stands at the replacement level." But of course, says the UNPD, the opposite is also true: "A relatively older age structure contributes to a slower rate of growth or, in more extreme cases, to population decline."[152] But for reasons unknown, at least to me, momentum does not factor into the UNPD's medium scenario.

> **NOTE:** Momentum helps explain why a country's overall population doesn't shrink right away when the fertility rate drops below the replacement rate. "You don't see the effects of fertility decreases until the last above-replacement generation dies," says Last.[153]

This is perplexing. Adding momentum to the modeling mix produces a very different outlook from other predictions. Specifically, under the momentum model, the global population reaches approximately 9 million people before stabilizing as early as 2050, much sooner than the UNPD's medium scenario would suggest. (See fig. 4.1.) But even these numbers seem off to me because the UNPD's momentum variant assumes constant mortality rates and instant replacement fertility rather than reflecting current and likely future trends in both these metrics. (I'll get into these trends later in this chapter.)

UN POPULATION PROJECTIONS (WPP 2022) - MEDIUM & MOMENTUM VARIANTS

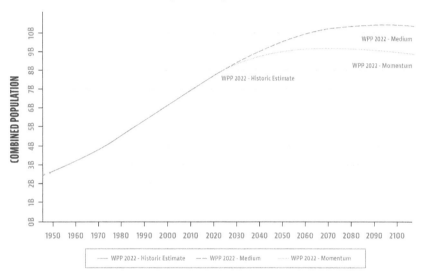

Figure 4.1. UN population projections: Medium and momentum variants
(Source: United Nations; graph generated by the author)

NOTE: I have concluded that biases, bureaucracy, and policy implications have prevented the UNPD from including the momentum variant in its more publicized projections and from calculating that variant using figures that reflect recent trends in fertility and mortality. What else could it be?

FORECASTS BY OTHER ORGANIZATIONS

The UNPD is the foremost authority on global demography. But it's far from the only authority. "In the past few years, rival groups have developed their own techniques and produced their own results," writes David Adam at *Nature*,[154] and these results are *very* different from the UNPD's. By and large, these groups believe the global population will peak earlier, and at a lower number, than the UNPD. I think they're right.

THE WITTGENSTEIN CENTRE

One such organization is the Wittgenstein Centre for Demography and Global Human Capital, a collaboration between the Austrian Academy of Sciences (ÖAW), the International Institute for Applied Systems Analysis (IIASA), and the University of Vienna.

In 2014 and again in 2018, the Wittgenstein Centre (WC-IIASA) performed its own population modeling. It used sex and age group data like the UNFP does. But it added a third element, education levels, to the mix—the theory being that the higher the educational level, the lower the fertility rate, and by extension the lower the projected population. In addition, rather than relying solely on historical data to forecast future trends, WC-IIASA researchers partnered with economists, sociologists, and demographers at the European Commission Joint Research Centre to weigh the effects of social, health, and economic factors on each country's development and population. They also identified pull and push factors likely to drive future trends in international migration.

Armed with this information, the WC-IIASA developed the following three population scenarios, which it called Social Scenario Pathways (SSPs):

- **SSP1:** The WC-IIASA describes SSP 1 as "the most optimistic scenario," with "rapid increases in life expectancy, a faster fertility decline in high fertility countries and an education expansion path that follows the education goals given by the SDGs (Sustainable Development Goals)."[155]

- **SSP3:** This scenario, says the WC-IIASA, is "a pessimistic scenario of stalled development." SSP3 "presents a divided world, foreseeing a stall in educational expansion in developing countries as well as continued high fertility and high mortality."[156]

- **SSP2:** This "medium" scenario "foresees that fertility and mortality follow a medium pathway,"[157] says the WC-IIASA. The WC-IIASA believes that SSP2, which it describes as "moderately optimistic," is the most likely scenario.

> **NOTE:** The SDGs are a collection of seventeen global goals devised by the United Nations General Assembly as a "shared blueprint for peace and prosperity for people and the planet, now and into the future."[158]

Assuming SSP2 does indeed materialize, the global population would continue to increase until sometime between 2070 and 2080. At that point it would crest somewhere around 9.8 billion people and then slowly decline to 9.5 billion people by 2100.[159] For comparison, recall that the UN medium scenario tops out at 10.431 billion in 2086 before declining to 10.349 billion in 2100.

INSTITUTE FOR HEALTH METRICS AND EVALUATION (IHME)

Another competing organization is the Institute for Health Metrics and Evaluation (IHME) at the University of Washington School of Medicine. Backed by the Bill & Melinda Gates Foundation, and using data from its 2017 Global Burden of Diseases, Injuries, and Risk Factors Study, the IHME took a fresh approach to population modeling in 2019.

Rather than using total fertility rate (like the UNPD does) in its calculations, IHME used a variable called *completed cohort fertility at age 50 years* (*CCF50*) to model fertility trends. "Because females tend to delay marriage and childbirth as they become more educated and enter the labour force," says the IHME, the total fertility rate "often declines and then increases, even though completed fertility over the course of a reproductive lifespan for any cohort of females is still declining or stagnant."[160]

In contrast, CCF50 "is much less affected by the delay of child-bearing that occurs as females become more educated." Moreover, it rarely increases, making it "much more stable."[161] Importantly, the IHME also included in its model variables to account for the underlying causes of changes in fertility rates, specifically education and the availability of contraceptives.

The IHME's conclusions, published in the *Lancet* in 2020, are very different from those of the UNPD's middle variant and slightly different from those of the WC-IIASA. In its *reference scenario*, which the IHME believes is the scenario most likely to play out, global population peaks in 2064 at 9.73 billion—far earlier than both the UNPD and the WC-IIASA predict—and drops to 8.79 billion by 2100.[162]

Table 4.2 shows how the forecasts from these three organizations—the UNPD (middle variant), the WC-IIASA, and the IHME—stack up.

Table 4.2. A comparison of forecasts from the UNPD (middle variant), WC-IIASA, and IHME

ORGANIZATION	2100 POPULATION (IN BILLIONS)	PEAK (IN BILLIONS) /YEAR
UNPD[163]	10.349	10.431/2086
WC-IIASA[164]	9.5	9.8/2070–2080
IHME[165]	8.79	9.73/2064

NOTE: Some established demographers have strenuously objected to the IHME's modeling approach and results. That's fair. But in my mind, the opinions of these demographers might hold more water if they acknowledged the shortcomings of their own modeling. When it comes to grappling with complicated issues such as population change, a little humility goes a long way!

THE EFFECTS OF COVID-19 ON THE GLOBAL POPULATION

At the time of this writing, in January 2023, more than 750 million cases of COVID-19 have been reported worldwide, resulting in nearly 7 million deaths.[166] This will almost certainly affect global fertility and population trends, although in different ways. For example, says David Adam at *Nature*,

"Demographers expect that the pandemic will cause a short-term dip in fertility, in richer countries at least, because of the associated economic uncertainty." But at the same time, "poorer countries could see a surge in pandemic births because of the disruption to contraception supplies."[167]

Still, here are a few things we *do* know:

- In China, births fell from 14.65 in 2019 to 12 million in 2020.[168] In 2021 they fell further to 10.6 million.[169] And in 2022 they fell further still to 9.56 million.[170] That's a difference of 5 million babies in just three years.
- The average birth rate in seventeen countries across Europe, Asia, and the United States fell by 5.1 percent in November 2020, 6.5 percent in December 2020, and 8.9 percent in January 2021 compared with the same months the previous year.[171]
- Of these seventeen countries, Spain sustained the sharpest drop: 20 percent in December 2020 and January 2021.[172]
- The date of peak global population might have moved forward by as much as a decade, into the 2050s.[173]
- Between 2019 and 2021, global life expectancy at birth fell from 72.8 years to 71.0 years.[174]

CURRENT TRENDS

Maybe you're not convinced about population decline. Fair enough. It's hard to see that many parts of the world will soon start shedding population when the total number of people continues to grow. But I assure you, it's coming. And in some places, it's already begun.

DECLINING FERTILITY RATES[175]

For proof of the coming demographic shift, one need look no further than fertility rates—a key leading indicator of future population trends. Figure 4.2 shows the precipitous drop in global fertility rates between 1950 and today and the UNPD's various projections for future fertility rates until 2100.

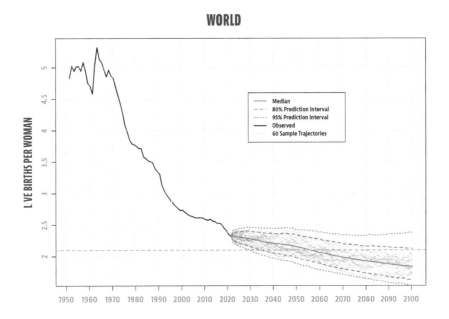

Figure 4.2. The drop in fertility rates from 1950 to the present day and UNPD projections until 2100 (Source: United Nations, DESA, Population Division)

Similarly, table 4.3 shows average fertility rates by region in 1950 and 2020 and projected fertility rates in 2050 and 2100, according to the UNPD.

NOTE: I used UNPD numbers here for the sake of example. I suspect fertility rates could fall even faster. But even what I consider to be conservative estimates show a dramatic drop in fertility rates!

Table 4.3. UNPD average fertility rates and projections (1950, 2021, 2050, 2100)[176]

REGION	AVERAGE FERTILITY RATE: 1950	AVERAGE FERTILITY RATE: 2020	AVERAGE FERTILITY RATE: 2050	AVERAGE FERTILITY RATE: 2100
Global	4.86	2.35	2.15	1.84
Africa	6.59	4.36	2.87	1.99
Asia	5.71	1.98	1.85	1.71
Europe	2.70	1.47	1.63	1.67
Latin America and the Caribbean	5.80	1.90	1.72	1.68
Oceania	3.67	2.16	1.96	1.77
North America	2.97	1.63	1.68	1.69

Even a cursory glance at this table reveals some startling truths:

- Global fertility has effectively fallen off a cliff since the early 1960s, although it went largely unnoticed, likely because of prevailing Malthusian views regarding the dangers of *over*population.

- Several areas are already below replacement rate, and if you set Africa aside, even those regions that *aren't* at replacement rate aren't far off.

- In 2100 every region on earth will be below replacement rate, including Africa.

> **NOTE:** Remember, the replacement fertility rate is 2.1.

But remember, I believe the UNPD's projections for 2050 and 2100 are high. One reason is that for the last twenty-plus years, the UNPD's medium variant has consistently overestimated fertility rates in advanced economies. However, it has also frequently *under*estimated fertility rates in emerging economies, so the result has effectively been a wash. Lately, though, fertility rates have fallen faster than predicted in emerging economies, and I don't see that changing. As that plays out, I expect fertility rates (and total population) to fall more, and sooner, than the UNPD medium variant would suggest.

> **NOTE:** The IHME also generally predicts fertility rates will decline more quickly than UNPD projections indicate, particularly on the global level. As noted in table 4.3, the UNPD projects that the global fertility rate will be 2.15 in 2050 and 1.84 in 2100; the IHME puts those numbers at 1.87 and 1.66, respectively.

The transition from high fertility to low fertility has not happened overnight. France's fertility rate began shifting downward in the late 1700s, even before Malthus drafted his famous screed warning of overpopulation. The fertility rates of other European countries eventually followed suit. At first, the descent was gradual. But now it's in freefall and nearing terminal velocity. Since the fall of the Berlin Wall in 1989, the fertility rate in Eastern Europe has plummeted to 1.43. Western Europe's fertility rate is higher, but not by much, at 1.63.

NOTE: Most Eastern European countries also run a negative migration balance, meaning more people emigrate *from* them than immigrate *to* them. These countries are hemorrhaging people.

Fertility rates in other parts of the world didn't dip as early as those in Europe. But they've fallen faster. Canada's fertility rate tumbled from 3.93 in 1959 to 1.46 in 2021. Similarly, in the United States, it plunged from 3.62 in 1957 to 1.66 in 2021 (although it did experience an upward bump between 1976 and 2007). By 2019, says economist Nicholas Eberstadt, "U.S. fertility levels were so low that even Mormon Utah had gone sub-replacement."[177] In the fourteen largest countries in Latin America, fertility rates have dropped "by the equivalent of half a baby since 2000," say Darrell Bricker and John Ibbitson in *Empty Planet.* This "isn't a gradual, smooth decline," they say. "This is collapse."[178]

In 1989 Japan sounded the alarm on its own declining fertility—an event called the "1.57 Shock" after that year's fertility rate. Despite Herculean efforts by the Japanese government to reverse this trend, the rate continued to decline. Since hitting its nadir at 1.27 in 2005, Japan's fertility has increased but only by a little bit: to 1.30 in 2021. To put this in perspective, Japan now produces more diapers for adults than it does for infants.

As low as Japan's fertility rate is, it's even lower in Taiwan (1.11) and Singapore (1.02). South Korea, though, has the lowest fertility rate of all. In 2021 the UNPD reported South Korea's fertility rate was 0.88. Since then, says Reuters, it's fallen further to 0.78.[179] And the rate in Seoul, the nation's capital, is even lower than that: 0.59. "How difficult must people find it to get married, give birth and raise children for this number to be so low?" mused Professor Lee Samsik of Hanyang University in Seoul. "If we take this as a compressed measure of basic life, it's a troublesome figure."[180]

No discussion of declining fertility would be complete without an examination of China. After the Chinese government implemented strict policies to limit births (discussed in chapter 2), the country's fertility rate tumbled from 5.52 in 1971 to 1.16 in 2021. "Even if the collapse is arrested and fertility remains at that level," says political economist Nicholas Eberstadt, "each new generation in China will be less than half as large as the one before it."[181]

As for China's BRICS brethren—Brazil, Russia, Indonesia, and South Africa—two remain above the replacement rate: Indonesia (2.18) and South Africa (2.37). But the others are below. In 2021 India's fertility rate was 2.03, Brazil's was 1.64, and Russia's was 1.49.

> **NOTE:** Here's a statistic. According to the UN, "In 2019, more than 40 percent of the world population lived in countries that were at or below the replacement rate of 2.1 children per woman; in 2021, this share climbed to 60 percent."[182]

All this is significant for one simple reason: once a country experiences low fertility for a sustained period, there's no going back. "Fertility trends have the turning radius of a battleship," says Last. "The further fertility drops, the more unbendable the downward trend becomes."[183]

HIGH-FERTILITY ZONES

There are, of course, a few areas in the world where fertility rates remain relatively high. One is Israel. In 2021 Israel boasted a fertility rate of 2.98, driven in part by very high birth rates among ultra-Orthodox Jews. Other parts of the Middle East and North Africa (MENA) region are similarly fecund, such as Yemen (3.80), Iraq (3.50), and Egypt (2.92). But sub-Saharan Africa experiences the highest fertility rates on earth, with Niger (6.82), Somalia (6.31), and the Democratic Republic of the Congo (6.16) topping the list.

Still, even in these high-fertility countries, birth rates are coming down—and much more quickly than expected. For example, recent data suggests that birth rates in Africa "are falling at a similar pace to those in some parts of Asia, when that region saw its own population growth rates slow sharply," says the *Economist*.[184] If this is true, says the Club of Rome— an influential think tank devoted to tackling problems on a global scale (and which itself warned against the dangers of overpopulation during the 1970s) predicts that the population of sub-Saharan Africa could peak as soon as 2060—forty years earlier than UN projections.[185]

SLOWING POPULATION GROWTH

If declining fertility rates are a leading indicator of population decline, a lower population growth rate—that is, the annual change in a population due to births, deaths, and migration, expressed as a percentage—is an even stronger one.

The global population growth rate peaked at 2.27 percent in 1963, during the height of the baby boom. Since then it's gone the way of a black diamond ski slope: steeply down. In 2021 it was just 0.82 percent. This tells us that the global population is still growing but not by much—and considering recent fertility rates, not for long. If the IHME is correct (and I think it is), the global population growth rate will soon be a negative number, and population will begin to decline.

DECLINING POPULATION

Some countries already have negative population growth rates, meaning their populations are now in decline. Italy's population growth rate turned negative in 2014 and now stands at –0.41. Japan's, which turned negative in 2010, is even lower, at –0.54. And the entirety of Eastern Europe, which turned negative in 1993, is even lower than that, at –0.58.

In 2022 China's population shrank by 850,000 people. It was the first time since 1961 that the country's population contracted. Back then the drop in population was a result of "three years of famine caused by Mao Zedong's disastrous Great Leap Forward industrial policy, along with floods and drought," says Christian Shepherd of the *Washington Post*.[186] This time, though, extremely low birth rates are primarily to blame (although COVID-19 played a part too). Reversing this trend will be all but impossible. Indeed, the WC-IIASA predicts that China's population will shed nearly 120 million people by 2050 and an additional 500 million people by 2100.[187]

> **NOTE:** The contraction of China's population wasn't exactly a surprise. But it happened earlier than most demographers expected. "Leading Chinese scholars and the United Nations estimated as recently as 2019 that the downward trend would not begin until early in the 2030s," says Shepherd.[188]

Even more dramatic than China's drop in population is Russia's. Like all of Eastern Europe, Russia's population has been in steady decline since the collapse of the Soviet Union in 1991. "As soon as Russians became free," says Last, "they suddenly, and without any explanation, stopped making babies."[189] Between October 2020 and September 2021, Russia's population shrank by just shy of a million people—its "largest natural population decline since World War II," says Brent Peabody at *Foreign Policy*.[190] Yes, COVID-19 and Russia's invasion of Ukraine have affected its population numbers. But the main culprit is the country's low birth rate (1.49).[191]

Speaking of Ukraine, it has its own population woes to contend with. In 2021 Ukraine already had one of the lowest birth rates on the planet (1.16). That was *before* the Russian invasion. Ukrainian demographers now believe that by the end of 2023, the country's fertility rate could be more than halved, to 0.55.[192]

This is just the tip of the iceberg. If the IHME's report in the *Lancet* is correct, the population of twenty-three countries will drop by *at least* 50 percent by 2100 (see table 4.4)—a development the IHME study's lead scientist described as "jaw-dropping."[193] Unless these countries change course, and fast, they face nothing short of population collapse.

Table 4.4. Countries with the highest projected population decline[194]

COUNTRY	2017 POPULATION (IN MILLIONS)	2100 PROJECTED POPULATION (IN MILLIONS)	PROJECTED POPULATION LOSS (IN MILLIONS)	PERCENTAGE DECLINE
Latvia	1.95	0.43	−1.52	77.59%
El Salvador	6.09	1.43	−4.66	76.52%
Jamaica	2.78	0.85	−1.93	69.42%
United Arab Emirates	9.73	3.45	−6.28	64.54%
Bulgaria	7.05	2.62	−4.43	62.84%
Croatia	4.28	1.62	−2.66	62.15%
Ukraine	44.69	17.55	−27.14	60.73%
Cuba	11.38	4.52	−6.86	60.28%
Romania	19.43	7.77	−11.66	60.01%
Poland	38.39	15.42	−22.97	59.83%
Moldova	3.72	1.51	−2.21	59.41%
Bosnia and Herzegovina	3.40	1.42	−1.98	58.24%
Portugal	10.68	4.50	−6.18	57.87%
Bermuda	0.07	0.03	−0.04	57.14%
Saint Vincent and the Grenadines	0.11	0.05	−0.06	54.55%
Taiwan	23.58	10.89	−12.69	53.82%
Japan	128.36	59.72	−68.64	53.47%
Serbia	8.87	4.14	−4.73	53.33%
Slovakia	5.42	2.56	−2.86	52.77%
Sri Lanka	21.60	10.45	−11.15	51.62%
Thailand	70.63	34.66	−35.97	50.93%
Spain	46.39	22.91	−23.48	50.61%

> **NOTE:** Author Fred Pearce observes, "There have already been days when the world got smaller," specifically December 26, 2004, when a tsunami in the Indian Ocean killed a quarter of a million people. That figure, plus the normal daily death toll of about 160,000, far exceeded the estimated 370,000 new births that day.[195]

A POINT OF NO RETURN

As mentioned, the UNPD assumes that in the years to come, fertility rates in many low-fertility countries will rebound because those countries will address the constraints that currently prevent women from having more children. But I don't see it.

Few low-fertility countries seem focused on or even interested in addressing these constraints, primarily because of the high costs involved. But even if a country *did* manage to address these issues—if education and childcare and everything else associated with having and raising children weren't so expensive, if couples achieved work-life balance and shared household and family duties more evenly—I don't see a reversal of current trends in countries that currently (or will soon) experience low fertility for three main reasons: social liberalization, urbanization, and economic insecurity.

SOCIAL LIBERALIZATION

Demographer Peter McDonald suggests that one key cause of low fertility in developed nations is increased social liberalization, "characterized most importantly by at least partial fulfillment of women's claims for a greater level of gender equity in the distribution of returns from modernization, particularly through paid employment." However, he says, "Family-related institutions, especially the family itself, continue to be characterized by gender inequity."[196]

The central problem then is that "family formation involves greater risks for women than for men. Accordingly, women are wary about embarking upon marriage and childbearing if they do not feel confident about their ability to combine family with the other opportunities that have opened up for them, especially paid employment,"[197] says McDonald. Put more simply, "Once a woman is socialized to have an education and a career, she is socialized to have a smaller family," says demographer Wolfgang Lutz.[198]

The social liberalization experienced by many advanced economies has also weakened patriarchal social institutions—none more than the church. Historically, religious organizations have sought to control the reproductive behaviors of believers, encouraging procreation and in some cases even forbidding the use of contraceptives. But the number of believers is down, especially among young people. According to a 2018 study conducted by Pew Research Center, young adults are less likely to practice a religion, especially in countries in North America, Europe, and Latin America.[199] Similarly, a 2021 Gallup poll revealed that just 36 percent of American millennials belonged to a religious congregation.[200]

One study by the US Centers for Disease Control's National Center for Health Statistics revealed that "virtually 100 percent of the decline in fertility in the United States from 2012 to 2019 can be explained through a combination of two factors: growing numbers of religious women leaving the faith, along with declining birth rates among the nonreligious,"[201] says Lyman Stone, a research fellow at the Institute for Family Studies.

Family ties in socially liberalized societies are often weaker too, especially in urban environments. "Family members now constitute a smaller part of people's social interactions than at any time in our evolutionary history," says psychologist Ilan Shira. Shira calls this development "the critical factor in decreasing birth rates" because "family members encourage each other to have children, whereas non-kin don't."[202]

Finally, social liberalization has given rise to increased individualism at the expense of communalism. Pearce puts it this way: "Individuals and society are pulling in different directions—and individuals are winning."[203] This shift in values favors concepts such as self-actualization and personal autonomy and prioritizes leisure time. As a result, say Bricker and Ibbitson, "Couples no longer see having children as a duty they must perform to satisfy their obligation to their families or their god. Rather, they choose to raise a child as an act of personal fulfillment. And they are quickly fulfilled."[204]

URBANIZATION

Chapter 2 mentioned that for the first time ever, urban dwellers outnumber rural ones. Many of these city folk are young people. Some are drawn to urban areas by educational and employment opportunities, others by cultural offerings and amenities, and still others by the adventure that awaits them. Importantly, chapter 2 also mentioned that people in cities typically experience lower fertility than people in rural areas. So as more and more young people move to cities, they will likely produce fewer children than they might have otherwise.

The effects of this shift will become increasingly pronounced in the coming years. According to the UN, the world's urban population is expected to skyrocket from 55 percent in 2018 to 68 percent in 2050, with India, China, and Nigeria accounting for 35 percent of this projected growth.[205] Many will migrate to one of forty-three projected megacities—that is, cities with more than 10 million inhabitants. But smaller cities, with fewer than 1 million inhabitants, are expected to proliferate too.[206] This will almost certainly result in significant declines in fertility rates.

ECONOMIC INSECURITY

The last thirty years have been a boon for companies and for individuals who were already wealthy. But in the United States and some other advanced economies, it's been a period during which many people, particularly in the working class, have experienced significant economic insecurity.

"Economic uncertainty is a powerful form of birth control,"[207] say Bricker and Ibbitson. Demographer Carl Haub agrees: "There is a good bit of evidence that hard economic times cause people to delay having babies or not to have one altogether." Particularly in places where the cost of living is prohibitively expensive, and among groups who carry significant debt (especially student debt), many young people feel they simply can't afford kids. Worse, by the time many women finally gain their financial footing and can begin contemplating starting a family, they're often well into their thirties or even their forties, when their biology tends to be less inclined to comply with their maternal desires.

LOW FERTILITY: THE "NEW NORMAL"

As societies become more socially liberalized, as populations become more urbanized, and as more and more young people in developed countries continue to experience economic insecurity, we can expect low fertility to become the "new normal." This trend will be very difficult, if not impossible, to reverse. "Once a country drops below childbirth replacement levels," writes Daniel F. Rundle at the Center for Strategic and International Studies (CSIS), "it almost never rises back to or above such levels again."[208] Moreover, says McDonald, "The longer low fertility is maintained, the harder it becomes to reverse population decline."[209] The math just doesn't work.

"Once global population decline begins," say the researchers at the IHME, "it will probably continue inexorably."[210] It will never, ever end.

CHAPTER 5

THE GOOD NEWS ABOUT POPULATION DECLINE

The 21st century will see a revolution in
the story of our human civilization.

—DR. RICHARD HORTON, EDITOR IN CHIEF OF THE *LANCET*

T hroughout the developed world, and even in some emerging economies, the fertility rate has dropped well below replacement levels. This can only mean one thing: our global population will decline—and much sooner than many people realize. Some countries are *already* experiencing population declines.

Whenever it happens, the effects of global population decline will be significant. But they won't be all bad. I believe population decline could have a considerable upside. That's what this chapter is about.

LOWER CARBON EMISSIONS

A shrinking human population will likely have a positive impact on the environment. To quote the IHME report in the *Lancet*, "Fewer people on the planet in every year between now and 2100 than the number forecasted by the UNPD would mean less carbon emission, less stress on global food systems, and less likelihood of transgressing planetary boundaries."[211] All good things!

Let's focus on the issue of carbon emission. Less carbon emission—that is to say lower levels of carbon dioxide (CO_2)—would certainly be welcome. Climate scientists overwhelmingly agree that rising CO_2 levels, from 278 parts per million (PPM) at the dawn of the Industrial Revolution to 419 PPM today,[212] is *the* underlying cause of climate change. Those same scientists predict that climate change will (and in some cases already has) cause rising seas,

> **A shrinking human population will likely have a positive impact on the environment.**

stronger and more frequent storms, more intense heat waves, changes in precipitation patterns, droughts, and a prolonged wildfire season. Disasters associated with climate change will likely displace human populations and increase homelessness, poverty, violence, and disease.

Rising CO_2 levels didn't just happen out of nowhere. The near-total consensus among climate scientists is that human behaviors and activities have largely driven this trend. According to the Union of Concerned Scientists (UCS), "Climate change is caused by the heat-trapping emissions produced when we burn coal, oil, and gas, and cut down forests."[213] The Intergovernmental Panel on Climate Change agrees: "Evidence is overwhelming that the climate has indeed changed since the pre-industrial era and that human activities are the principal cause of that change."[214]

The rise in CO2 levels has occurred in tandem with the rise in the human population. So it's reasonable to predict that as our human population declines, CO2 emissions will decline in kind. This was the finding of one 2017 study, which predicted that if the UN's low-variant population model were to prove accurate—and I believe it, or something like it, will—then per capita emissions would drop 10 percent by 2055 and 35 percent by 2100.[215]

Another 2017 study concluded that the most impactful thing an individual in the developed world could do to fight climate change would be to have one fewer child. Researchers calculated that this decision, albeit a radical one, could reduce a person's annual carbon footprint by more than 58 tonnes per year (TPY). This far exceeds reductions associated with other climate-friendly behaviors such as living car-free (2.4 TPY), consuming a plant-based diet (0.8 TPY), and avoiding air travel (1.6 tonnes per round-trip transatlantic flight).[216]

Interestingly, just as population decline would appear to influence climate change, climate change seems likely to affect population decline—or more specifically, fertility rates. In 2020 the academic journal *Climatic Change* reported that when more than 600 Americans between the ages of twenty-seven and forty-five were asked whether they factored climate change into their reproductive choices, their answer was a resounding *yes*. "96.5 of respondents were 'very' or 'extremely concerned' about the well-being of their existing, expected, or hypothetical children in a climate-changed world."[217] Analysts at Morgan Stanley agree, so much so that in July 2021, they warned investors that a "movement to not have children owing to fears over climate change is growing and impacting fertility rates quicker than any preceding trend in the field of fertility decline."[218]

Climate change, or more precisely the environmental degradation associated with climate change, could influence fertility rates in another way too by decreasing fertility from a biological standpoint. For instance, a 2021 study in China found that particulate pollution increased the likelihood of infertility by 20 percent.[219]

> **NOTE:** Some people, called anti-natalists, promote the notion that no one should have any children, ever, for moral reasons. Their goal is the complete extinction of humankind for the sake of the planet.

Not everyone believes population decline will rein in climate change. This is because global population is just one of three main inputs in the climate change equation. The other two are as follows:

- How much each person consumes

- How much CO2 is emitted to support each person's consumption

Many climate scientists assert that consumption, not population, is the critical cause of climate change. "A misplaced focus on population growth as a key driver of past, present, and future climate change conflates a rise in emissions with an increase in people, rather than the real source of those emissions," say members of the UCS. This *real* source, they say, is "an increase in cars, power plants, airplanes, industries, buildings, and other parts of our fossil fuel-dependent economy and lifestyles."[220] In other words, consumption.

I'm not sure they're right. Not everyone on earth consumes the same amount. Some people consume very little, while others consume a lot. Correspondingly, the CO2 emissions from some people's consumption are minuscule, while the emissions from others are quite substantial. To illustrate, table 5.1 breaks down CO_2 emissions by continent. (Note that this table includes the Arabian Peninsula too, even though it is not a continent, because its emissions are noteworthy.)

Table 5.1. 2020 per capita and total CO2 emissions (in tonnes) by continent[221]

CONTINENT	PER CAPITA CO2 EMISSIONS IN 2020	TOTAL POPULATION IN 2020	TOTAL CO2 EMISSIONS IN 2020
Africa	0.99	1,340,598,111	1,326,043,539
South America	2.31	430,759,771	994,160,327
Asia	4.38	4,639,847,425	20,317,058,379
Europe	6.67	748,843,405	4,946,034,489
North America	9.81	592,062,319	4,946,034,489
Australia	15.37	25,499,881	391,891,928
Arabian Peninsula	17.70	88,490,063	1,078,257,036

These numbers reveal something significant: wealthier parts of the world have much higher per capita CO_2 emissions than poorer areas. The data in table 5.2 supports this conclusion. So does research by Oxfam and the Stockholm Environment Institute. These organizations calculated that the richest 10 percent of the global population is responsible for 52 percent of carbon emissions, while the poorest 50 percent is responsible for just 7 percent.[222]

Table 5.2. 2020 per capita and total CO2 emissions (in tonnes) by income level[223]

INCOME LEVEL	PER CAPITA CO2 EMISSIONS	TOTAL CO2 EMISSIONS
Low-income countries	0.24	156,818,079
Lower-middle-income countries	1.75	5,825,886,924
Upper-middle-income countries	6.22	15,895,921,988
High-income countries	9.78	11,828,815,872

Fertility is dropping most dramatically in upper-middle- and high-income countries, and the total population of these countries will soon follow suit. When this happens, the total CO2 emissions from these countries will likewise fall, even if the per capita emissions don't, because the group of people who consume the most will become smaller.

Of course, when it comes to addressing climate change, time is of the essence. And unfortunately, lower emissions due to population decline won't materialize quickly enough to stabilize the climate all on their own. Nations, industries, and individuals must continue with efforts to reduce emissions through other means. "Reducing human impact on the environment through reduced per capita consumption of energy and materials, in tandem with developing more sustainable production processes, is significantly more likely to produce meaningful impacts," say economists Melissa Kearney and Philip Levine of the Aspen Institute.[224]

MORE PLENTIFUL RESOURCES

Carbon emission is just one measure of our impact on the environment. Another is our ecological footprint. To quote the Global Footprint Network (GFN), our *ecological footprint* "tracks how much biologically productive land and water area an individual, population or activity uses to produce all the resources it consumes, to house all its infrastructure, and to absorb its waste given prevailing technology and resource management practices."[225]

Before 1970 our ecological footprint (the amount of nature we used) was less than our biocapacity (the amount of nature we had). So we had an ecological reserve. But in the half century since, we've been running an ecological deficit—using more nature than we have.

As you might guess, one reason for this ecological deficit is that our ecological footprint has grown. Because of the aforementioned increase in "cars, power plants, industries, buildings, and other parts of our fossil fuel-dependent economy and lifestyles," we use more nature than we used to. But there's another reason: because of the effects of climate change, a growing human population, and human behaviors and activities such as deforestation, overfarming, and overfishing, our biocapacity has shrunk. In 1970 our per capita ecological footprint and our per capita biocapacity were the same: 2.72 global hectares (gha). In 2018 they were 2.77 gha and 1.58 gha, respectively.

> **NOTE:** The purpose of the ecological footprint is to assess resource use and sustainability. The GFN expresses sustainability by the number of earths required to sustain our ecological footprint. In 2023 this number was 1.75. Earth Overshoot Day, the day the earth exhausted its resources and began running an ecological deficit, was July 28.

Just as people in the wealthiest countries have the highest per capita CO2 emissions, they have the biggest per capita ecological footprints too. Crucially, many of these countries also operate at an ecological deficit. That is, their per capita biocapacity is lower than their per capita ecological footprint. So they ravage resources cultivated elsewhere, usually in poorer countries.

To provide a representative sample, table 5.3 shows the per capita ecological footprint, biocapacity, and ecological reserve or deficit of nations in the Group of 20 (G20). (Data for the European Union as a whole, which is part of the G20, was not available.) As you can see, all but five of these countries run an ecological deficit, with Saudi Arabia (–4.6), the United States (–4.7), and South Korea (–5.7) being the worst offenders.

Table 5.3. 2018 per capita ecological footprint, biocapacity, and reserve or deficit (in global hectares) of G20 countries[226]

COUNTRY	PER CAPITA ECOLOGICAL FOOTPRINT	PER CAPITA BIOCAPACITY	PER CAPITA RESERVE/DEFICIT
Argentina	3.3	6.2	+2.9
Australia	7.1	11.5	+4.4
Brazil	2.7	9.5	+6.8
Canada	8.1	14.7	+6.6
China	3.8	0.9	−2.9
France	4.5	2.4	−2.1
Germany	4.7	1.5	−3.2
India	1.2	0.4	−0.8
Indonesia	1.7	1.2	−0.5
Italy	4.3	0.8	−3.5
Japan	4.6	0.6	−4.0
Mexico	2.4	1.2	−1.2
Russia	5.3	6.7	+1.4
Saudi Arabia	5.0	0.4	−4.6
South Africa	3.8	1.0	−2.8
South Korea	6.3	0.6	−5.7
Turkey	3.3	1.3	−2.0
United Kingdom	4.2	1.0	−3.2
United States	8.1	3.4	−4.7

Just as total CO_2 emissions will likely drop as populations decline, so will demand for natural resources because the countries that consume the most natural resources (upper-middle- and high-income countries) will experience the most dramatic drops in population. And as with CO2 emissions, even if per capita ecological foot-prints remain relatively high in wealthier nations, their total ecological footprints will drop because the number of people who consume the most will shrink. Ultimately, as human pressures on our environment ease, biocapacity will improve, resulting in a healthier, more sustainable planet. "In a world of limited resources and major environmental problems," says economist Paul Krugman, "there's something to be said for a reduction in population pressure."[227]

> **TIP:** Firms that develop products to reduce our environmental footprint or improve our biocapacity are ripe for investment. These include companies that focus on solutions driven by market needs in areas such as renewable energy, energy efficiency, and sustainable agriculture.

INCOME AND WEALTH EQUALITY

People don't just compete for resources. They compete for jobs too. Until very recently, competition for jobs has been particularly fierce, for one simple reason: the global labor force more than doubled after the early 1990s. This positive labor shock was the result of a confluence of events, including the rise of China in world trade, the collapse of the Soviet Union and subsequent reemergence of Eastern Europe in world trade, baby boomers reaching peak working age, and more women entering the labor force, among others.

Positive labor shocks are great for employers, especially when coupled with globalization. Suddenly, the pool of potential employees expands from local laborers to workers all over the world, most of whom are willing to work for much lower wages. So employers pay less for labor, rake in more profits, and their wealth grows.

But positive labor shocks coupled with globalization are notoriously *bad* for workers, at least for workers in more advanced economies. Plentiful labor on a global scale weakens their bargaining power, limits their wages, and perhaps prevents them from landing a job at all.

> **NOTE:** Workers in emerging economies fare better in these conditions. Although they earn less than employees in advanced economies, they generally earn more than they might if employed by a local operation.

In advanced economies, one inevitable outcome of positive labor shocks is increasing inequality in both income and wealth. This is certainly true in the United States. According to the Economic Policy Institute, annual wages for the bottom 90 percent of American earners increased by only 28.2 percent between 1979 and 2020. In contrast, earners in the top 10 percent cleared 83.1 percent more in annual wages, the top 1 percent pulled in 179.3 percent more, and the top 0.1 percent reaped 389.1 percent more.[228]

According to the World Inequality Lab (WIL), a research organization founded by economist Thomas Piketty to study the effects of inequality, the United States is not alone. In every major region of the world (save Europe), the bottom 50 percent of earners collect less than 15 percent of total wages. That number is even worse for earners in Latin America, sub-Saharan Africa, and the Middle East, whose share is less than 10 percent. In contrast, the top 10 percent of earners haul in more than 40 percent in total wages; in some regions, that number is closer to 60 percent.

The difference is even starker when comparing wealth. The WIL estimates that the bottom 50 percent of people possess just 2 percent of total global wealth, while the top 10 percent control 76 percent. "Since wealth is a major source of future economic gains, and increasingly, of power and influence, this presages further increases in inequality," says the WIL.[229]

I believe this is about to change. In fact, this alteration might already be underway. This is because many of the factors that contributed to the surge in available labor—in particular, China's ascendance, the collapse of the Soviet Union and the reemergence of Eastern Europe, and the surge in baby boomers reaching peak working age—have begun to reverse.

Let's start with China. In 2016 its working-age population was just under 1 billion people. By 2022 that number had dropped to 983 million.[230] China shed 17 million working-age people in *six years*. As bad as this sounds for China, things are about to get even worse as the consequences of the country's catastrophic one-child policy continue to manifest. According to UN projections, China's working-age population will shed an additional 216 million people by 2050.[231] (That's roughly the population of Nigeria!) But remember, UN projections are notoriously conservative. Moreover, China's total population shrank by 850,000 people in 2022, a decade earlier than expected. It's reasonable to assume that the country's workforce will contract even more, and sooner, than predicted.

Things aren't much rosier in Eastern Europe. Populations throughout this region are also set to decline and in some cases already have. One reason is emigration. "The ex-communist countries that joined the European Union from 2004 on dreamed of quickly transforming themselves into Germany or Britain," says the *Economist*. "Instead, many of their workers transported themselves to Germany or Britain."[232] But low fertility rate is also an issue. According to UNFPA, "Even the high-fertility variant of UN population projections still foresees population numbers going down by 2060 in many countries in the region."[233]

And what of the baby boomers? Well, let's just say they're not getting any younger. At the time of this writing, the youngest members of this group are fifty-nine years old. As for the oldest members, they're seventy-seven. Most baby boomers have already aged out of the workforce, and the ones that haven't aren't far behind.

As these developments unfold, and as the labor pool contracts, workers will gain more bargaining power, and "real wages and the relative income share of labour will start rising again," say economists Charles Goodhart and Manoj Pradhan in *The Great Demographic Reversal*. (Relative income describes one's earnings as compared with the average income.) When that happens, they say, "Labor will reclaim a greater share of national input."[234] In other words inequality will fall.

> **NOTE:** On a related note, lower fertility rates free up more women to work. This could have an enormous economic upside in emerging economies because "More people working should boost prosperity," says the *Economist*. They cite a 2017 study that revealed that "lowering the fertility rate by one child per woman in Nigeria could almost double personal income by 2060."[235]

BETTER JOBS FOR NATIVE-BORN WORKERS AND MORE MOBILITY FOR MIGRANTS

Recent years have seen pronounced anti-immigrant sentiment among the inhabitants of many advanced economies. Those who hold these views cite various reasons. In the United States, for example, Americans who oppose immigration might say it's because immigrants commit more crimes, or because they don't want to assimilate into American culture, or because they're a drain on government resources (such as welfare and other government benefits), or because they just don't like them. More often, though, they claim it's because immigrants steal good jobs from hardworking Americans. (Many of these same Americans also claim that immigrants are lazy and don't want to work, prompting one cheeky pundit to coin the term "Schrödinger's immigrant.")

These anti-immigrant attitudes have led many Americans to support politicians who are similarly disposed, the most notable being former president Donald J. Trump, who launched his 2016 presidential campaign by claiming that Mexican immigrants were "bringing drugs. They're bringing crime. They're rapists." Trump's subsequent election allowed for the implementation of government policies to significantly limit immigration.

> **NOTE:** The United States is hardly the only country to become increasingly anti-immigrant in recent years. Extreme far-right political parties have gained traction in many parts of the world. Chapter 9 discusses this trend in more detail.

It's true that for the last few decades, many Americans, as well as workers in other advanced economies, have faced dwindling job prospects and declining wages. But it's not because of immigrants. It's because of the positive labor shock discussed in the preceding section. As their population and labor pool contracts, they'll have more opportunities to find good jobs that suit them—something they actually *like*, that has dignity and meaning—and to earn more money doing them. Advanced education could also become both more accessible and less expensive, perhaps even free.

A contracting labor pool also enables often overlooked and underrepresented populations, such as women and minorities, to realize their potential as good jobs previously denied them become available. Here in the United States, a push for this has already begun. In February 2023 US Secretary of Commerce Gina Raimondo called on employers to attract women and members of other underserved communities to elevate the US workforce into "the most diverse, productive, and talented workers in the world."[236] When this happens, these populations will even be able to command equal pay for equal work—finally.

For some types of jobs—menial jobs that are tedious, are repetitive, and involve lots of drudgery—automation, robotics, and artificial intelligence (AI) will pick up the slack. Work that is more complex and requires more intelligence, however, will still need to be performed by human beings. If there aren't enough native-born laborers in a country to do that work—that is, if there are too many jobs but not enough people—then that country will need immigrants. So for people in developing nations, where there are often plenty of people but not enough jobs, opportunities to seek a better life elsewhere will abound.

This development will be a win-win. As workers emigrate from countries with too many people but not enough jobs, they'll free up positions for those workers who remain, potentially providing social mobility for groups that have long languished in poverty.

Eventually, so many rich countries will need immigrants so badly they'll have to compete to attract them. This competition will become even more intense as our demographic contagion infects the developing countries from which many immigrants hail, causing their own fertility rates to drop below replacement levels and their own populations to age and decline too.

NOTE: I'll talk more about immigration in chapter 9.

IMPROVED QUALITY OF LIFE

All these developments—lower carbon emissions, more plentiful resources, income and wealth equality, more opportunities for women and minorities, and more mobility for immigrants—will have compounding positive effects on our quality of life. For example,

- **Improved health:** Ground-level ozone and fine particulate matter associated with carbon emissions can cause asthma, heart and lung disease, and cancer and lead to premature death. So reducing them will improve health. Reducing emissions will also help avert negative health outcomes associated with the effects of climate change, such as rising seas, severe storms, extreme heat exposure, wildfires, changes in precipitation patterns, droughts, a prolonged wildfire season, and new disease vectors.

- **Less conflict:** A smaller population, combined with more ccological reserves, will result in less competition for valuable natural resources. This will yield a more peaceful planet, as fewer groups will need to fight each other simply to sustain themselves.

- **Increased happiness:** Income and wealth inequality are linked to a great many social ills: more crime, less social mobility, increased stress and anxiety, poor health, a lack of trust and engagement, and lower social and civic participation. More simply, it makes people unhappy. By improving equality, we increase our happiness.

- **A thriving society:** Societies thrive when *everyone* is free to seek and reach their potential, women and minorities included.

- **A richer culture:** Immigration doesn't just improve the lives of immigrants. Welcoming immigrants promotes a richer culture—one that integrates new ideas, expertise, customs, cuisines, and art with the existing culture—from which everyone benefits.

CHAPTER 6

THE BAD NEWS ABOUT POPULATION DECLINE

Population collapse is potentially the greatest risk to the future of civilization.

—ELON MUSK, BUSINESS MAGNATE AND INVESTOR

I believe population decline will yield some positive outcomes—lower carbon emissions, more plentiful resources, less income inequality, better jobs for native-born workers (including women and other traditionally underrepresented groups), more mobility for immigrants, and improved quality of life. But unfortunately, many of these outcomes will be overshadowed by the negative consequences of population decline.

I divide the negative consequences associated with population decline into two main categories: economic and social. But both these categories relate to the same underlying issue: aging populations due to low fertility rates. This chapter delves into this underlying issue, and into the associated negative consequences, in detail.

AGING POPULATIONS

In 1950 the median age on planet Earth was 23.6 years. In 2020 it was 30.9. As shown in table 6.1, the last 70 years have brought increases in the median age of human populations across every continent.

Table 6.1. Changes in median age by region (1950–2020)[237]

REGION	MEDIAN AGE 1950	MEDIAN AGE 2020	RELATIVE CHANGE
Africa	18.1	18.6	+2%
Asia	20.6	30.8	+50%
Europe	27.8	41.5	+49%
Latin America/ Caribbean	18.3	29.9	+63%
North America	29.0	37.7	+30%
Oceania	26.4	31.9	+21%

When you examine these numbers country by country, the increases are often much more extreme. Table 6.2 provides several examples.

Table 6.2. Changes in median age in select countries (1950–2020)[238]

COUNTRY	MEDIAN AGE 1950	MEDIAN AGE 2020	RELATIVE CHANGE
Brazil	17.5	32.4	+86%
China	22.2	37.4	+68%
Germany	33.4	44.9	+35%
Italy	27.5	46.4	+69%
India	20.0	27.3	+36%
Japan	21.2	48.0	+126%
Qatar	17.6	32.0	+82%
Russia	23.4	38.6	+65%
Saudi Arabia	17.9	32.0	+64%
South Africa	19.2	26.9	+40%
South Korea	17.6	42.8	+142%
Spain	26.5	43.5	+64%
United Kingdom	33.9	39.5	+16%
United States	29.3	37.5	+28%
Venezuela	16.1	27.8	+72%

One obvious reason for this increase in median age is the corresponding increase in the human life span. Thanks to advances in science and medicine, the average human life span more than doubled between 1900 (32.0 years) and 2000 (66.5 years), peaking at 72.8 years in 2019.[239] (It has since dropped slightly due mainly to the effects of the COVID-19 pandemic.)

THE EVER-EXPANDING HUMAN LIFE SPAN

Many futurists believe that further scientific advances could add 30 or more healthy years to the human life span. "Imagine having the cognition, esthetics and mobility at 100 years old that you had at 60," says futurist Peter Diamandis.[240] While this all sounds wonderful, there is one downside: it will result in an even higher global median age.

Median age is also influenced by another key input: fertility rate. As you've learned, fertility rates are plummeting and in many areas are well below replacement rate. So there are fewer young people to draw the median age back down.

Some demographers conservatively predict a global median age of 41.9 in the year 2100[241]—a 77 percent jump over today's level. The key word here is *conservatively*. I see evidence that the global median age will increase even more and quite a bit sooner. We are facing what many demographers call a "silver tsunami."

NOTE: The UN projects that by 2050, the median age in the United States will be 43.[242] That's older than Florida's median age now (42.4).[243] You know, Florida. Where practically everyone's retired.

As the median age of a population rises, it affects that population's old-age dependency ratio (OADR). This widely used metric compares the number of older people (dependents) in a population with the number of younger people (producers). The OADR, which generally defines "older people" as people aged 65 and up and "younger people" as people aged 15 to 64, is calculated like this:

$$\text{Old Age Dependency Ratio} = \frac{\text{(Dependents)}}{\text{(Producers)}} \times 100$$

Populations with a low OADR have lots of working-age people (producers) to support the older people (dependents). But in populations with a high OADR, there are relatively fewer working-age people to carry that load. That's bad.

> **NOTE:** The OADR for a specific population changes if its mortality rate changes, its fertility rate changes, and people immigrate to or emigrate from the area where that population lives.

Historically, most countries have had a low OADR. These days, though, not so much. Table 6.3 shows the OADR for the same countries listed in table 6.2 between 1960 and 2020. Only Qatar and Saudi Arabia have a lower OADR today than they did in 1960.

Table 6.3. Changes in the OADR (1960–2020)[244]

COUNTRY	OADR 1960	OADR 2020	RELATIVE CHANGE
Brazil	4.3	13.3	+206%
China	8.4	18.2	+117%
Germany	14.2	34.2	+141%
India	5.3	9.9	+89%
Italy	12.4	36.7	+196%
Japan	8.2	50.6	+517%
Qatar	6.5	1.5	−77%
Russia	7.3	22.8	+213%
Saudi Arabia	6.1	3.3	−45%
South Africa	7.3	9.2	+27%
South Korea	5.0	22.0	+335%
Spain	10.9	29.8	+174%
United Kingdom	16.3	29.5	+81%
United States	12.6	24.9	+97%
Venezuela	4.4	12.6	+187%

To put the ever-rising OADR into context, consider that in 1950 the United States had 7.9 producers for each elder dependent. By 2020 that number was halved to 4.0 producers per elder dependent. By 2035 it's expected to drop even further, to under three producers per elder dependent.[245] As the number of young people continues to drop relative to the number of old people, and current data indicates that it will, there will be grave economic and social consequences.

> **NOTE:** Although falling fertility rates mean there will be fewer working-age adults relative to the number of older people, there will also be "more working-age adults relative to the number of children, says the *Economist*.[246] This could help ease some of the pressures associated with aging societies.

ECONOMIC IMPACTS

A rising OADR results in too few workers, producing too few goods and services. This has a variety of profound economic effects on the general economy and on government operations.

First, let's talk about "too few workers." Back in 2008 the UN estimated that the US working-age population would reach 230 million people in 2030. But a 2015 report by the same organization revised this estimate downward, to 217 million.[247] That's 13 million fewer workers than expected. But even this revised estimate is likely too high, as it does not account for the increased mortality rate due to the recent COVID-19 pandemic—a number that Federal Reserve Jerome Powell placed at "close to half a million" in December 2022.[248]

The United States is not unique. Regions all over the world are experiencing the same trends that will inevitably reduce their working-age population. In Europe this contraction has already begun. Researchers at the Federal Reserve Bank of St. Louis estimate that the working-age population in the European Union fell from 334 million in 2009 to 327 million in 2019.[249]

Things are even more dire in China. Apart from the fact that its total population recently contracted for the first time in four decades, China shed 17 million working-aged people between 2016 and 2022 and is expected to hemorrhage an additional 216 million by 2050.[250] This is *unprecedented*.

These are just a few examples of countries facing a contraction in their labor pool. The fact is, to a greater or lesser degree, this is the looming future of virtually every developed country on earth.

EFFECTS ON THE GENERAL ECONOMY

Many countries will soon (if they don't already) face having too few people, producing too few goods and services. But what does that *mean*? There are a few possible answers.

One answer is that a shrinking labor force could result in decreased productivity. This is just basic math: fewer workers generally equals less output. Advancements in technology could mitigate this, but whether they will mitigate it enough, and in time, is a matter of debate.

Here's another answer: because there will be fewer workers, those workers who remain will be in a position to command higher wages. That's great for those workers, but it will likely also result in lower profit margins for businesses and higher prices for consumers.

If higher prices cancel out gains in wages, demand for consumer goods among working-age people could fall. Demand will fall even further in societies with significantly more older people than younger people because, says the IHME, "Many retirees are less likely to purchase consumer durables than middle-aged and young adults."[251]

Then there's this: a shrinking labor pool could drive up inflation. This is the central thesis of Goodhart and Pradhan's book: that due in large part to a quickly contracting workforce, "the world will increasingly shift from a deflationary bias to one in which there is a major inflationary bias."[252] Indeed, it seems this shift has already begun, although most economists attribute it to surging demand, supply chain issues, production costs, and government relief funds during the COVID-19 pandemic rather than to limited labor. Still, a contracting labor pool won't help matters; it will just make things worse. Worse, because of the number of complex and interrelated inflationary pressures in play, once inflation starts, it's very hard to stop, and any attempts to do so typically require radical action that is extremely painful in the short term.

Rising inflation doesn't just drive up prices. It also affects interest rates because raising interest rates is the primary tool that central banks use to reduce inflation. This isn't necessarily a bad thing. If you've stashed a bunch of money in a savings account, then rising interest rates will benefit you. But companies (and people) that rely on low-interest loans or credit simply to sustain operations will find themselves exposed. (To quote Warren Buffett, "You only learn who has been swimming naked when the tide goes out."[253]) Rising interest rates aren't great for housing markets either because of higher borrowing costs.

> **NOTE:** Speaking of the housing market, what will happen to it once population starts to decline? If fewer houses are needed, will real estate depreciate, the way a used car does? And what about the companies that construct homes? "If the number of families is declining, there's not much need to build new housing," says economist Paul Krugman.[254]

INFLATION INTEREST RATES AND DEBT

The issue here isn't so much about how much debt a company already holds (assuming they assumed that debt at a fixed interest rate). In fact, with inflation, that debt might even be easier to pay off than it would have been otherwise because the value of the currency when the company acquired the debt was less than the value of the currency with inflation. However, for companies that need to take on new debt just to stay afloat, inflation and higher interest rates make things *much* harder.

Investment patterns and capital flows will likely change too. "Older people want fixed income and are more risk-averse," says Daniel Rundle at the CSIS. "This risk aversion will impact the amount of risk capital in a society, thereby reducing the capital available for entrepreneurs."[255]

In the end this might not matter much because according to demographer Phillip Longman in *The Empty Cradle*, "After the proportion of elders increases in a society beyond a certain point, the level of entrepreneurship and inventiveness decreases."[256] So that's a lose-lose.

The combination of decreased productivity, lower profit margins, higher prices, lower demand for consumer goods, rising inflation, rising interest rates, and reduced capital for entrepreneurs ... will limit growth.

One thing is certain: the combination of decreased productivity, lower profit margins, higher prices, lower demand for consumer goods, rising inflation, rising interest rates, and reduced capital for entrepreneurs—all due at least in part to aging or declining populations—will limit growth. Growth won't just slow down, though. In some places it will *reverse*. GDP will go down not just for a quarter or two but for years—maybe even forever.

This is new terrain. Negative nominal GDP growth is unheard of in our modern economy. There aren't even data modeling tools for a negative GDP! But one thing is clear: the effects will be dramatic … and bad. "Growth is not a cure-all," say Marian Tupy and Gale Pooley in their book *Superabundance*. "But lack of growth is a kill-all."[257]

EFFECTS ON GOVERNMENT OPERATIONS

The economic effects of a smaller labor pool will extend to government operations. One effect will be a limited ability to sustain popular services such as national health insurance and social security programs and to build and maintain infrastructure because fewer people will pay taxes. Another will be increased difficulty managing government debt.

Sustaining popular social services presents a particularly painful dilemma for politicians. Should they raise taxes? Or should they renege on promises made to elderly populations? This second option is frankly unthinkable, not just from a moral standpoint but from a pragmatic one too, at least in countries that operate as democracies, where the elderly comprise a considerable voting bloc. But increased taxation might not work either because it will disproportionately affect the young, who tend to drive economic growth. Besides, some countries "are [already] close to the limits of what tax policy can do to relieve the situation," say economists Burkhard Heer, Vito Polito, and Michael R. Wickens.[258] For these countries, the question is moot.

When it comes to managing government debt, rising interest rates pose a significant problem, particularly for governments that rely heavily on debt to sustain themselves. Eventually, some governments could even be forced to default on their debt, which would have far-reaching and compounding consequences. For example, in the United States, according to a 2021 communication issued by the White House,

> A default would fundamentally hinder the Federal government from serving the American people. Payments from the Federal government that families rely on to make ends meet would be endangered. The basic functions of the Federal government—including maintaining national defense, national parks, and countless others—would be at risk. The public health system, which has enabled this country to react to a global pandemic, would be unable to adequately function.
>
> Furthermore, a default would have serious and protracted financial and economic effects. Financial markets would lose faith in the United States, the dollar would weaken, and stocks would fall. The U.S. credit rating would almost certainly be downgraded, and interest rates would broadly rise for many consumer loans, making products like auto loans and mortgages more expensive for families who are subject to interest rate changes or taking out new loans. These and other consequences could trigger a recession and a credit market freeze that could hurt the ability of American companies to operate.[259]

If a country's government cannot offer essential services or pay its debts, that country will almost certainly face political instability and social unrest. By extension, it will also find itself in a weaker geopolitical position.

Countries with low fertility rates and aging or declining populations could find their geopolitical positions further undermined by an inability to maintain a strong fighting force, for the following three reasons:

- There will be a smaller pool of young people from which the military can recruit.

- According to Neil Howe and Richard Jackson at the CSIS, "Smaller families may be less willing to risk scarce youth in war."[260]

- Money that should go toward assembling a fighting force will be diverted to pay pensions for retired military personnel, at least in the short term.

The upshot: Older societies with fewer children "will find it difficult to project power in the wider world," says Jonathan V. Last in *What to Expect When No One's Expecting*.[261]

Fortunately, the geopolitical positions of *all* countries with aging and declining populations will be weakened, including notoriously belligerent countries such as China and Russia. And anyway, as societies age, they might naturally become less combative, as older electorates "shun decisive confrontations in favor of ad hoc settlements," say Howe and Jackson.[262] So the result could be a more peaceful and democratic world. One can hope, anyway.

EFFECTS ON SOCIETY

An aging or declining population has deleterious effects on a country's GDP. But the GDP of any country simply serves as a proxy measurement of that country's standard of living.

In recent decades the world has become accustomed to progress—the accumulation of wealth, better health and living conditions, advances in education, and so on. The key driver of this progress is inarguably economic growth, or increased GDP.

Declining GDP—or worse, a complete about-face—will reverse these advances. If an aging population reduces a country's GDP (and we've established that it does), it's fair to say that it also, by extension, affects the well-being of individuals within a society as well as the society at large.

To illustrate, consider that a society with more old people than young people will almost certainly lack adequate workers to care for the elderly population. There just won't be enough. And while some types of workers could eventually be replaced by machines or robots, care workers generally can't. "Care involves personal and emotional support,"[263] say Goodhart and Pradhan, something machines and robots can never provide.

Because of this shortfall in care workers, it will likely fall to families to care for their loved ones as they age. But this presents its own set of problems. If the population of a society is aging or declining, then the families within that population are almost certainly smaller than they used to be.

China is a perfect example. Historically, it has fallen to Chinese families to care for their elderly relatives. That wasn't so hard when families were large. But today because of China's one-child policy (in effect from 1980 until 2016), many working-age Chinese individuals are expected to care for both of their parents and all four of their grandparents while also working and perhaps raising children of their own—often with no siblings, cousins, aunts, uncles, or any other blood relatives to help them.

> **NOTE:** What about elderly members of society who don't have family to care for them? Often, they die alone. This has become "hauntingly common" in Japan, writes Justin Nobel in *Time* magazine.[264] There's even a Japanese word for it: *kodokushi*, or "lonely deaths."

Sociologists refer to working-age adults who care for their parents while also raising children as the "sandwich generation." Life for this group is extremely challenging, not to mention expensive and exhausting. A 2020 survey by the *New York Times* revealed that many members of the sandwich generation estimated they had lost more than $10,000 "because they had to do things like reduce their working hours, increase their expenses or leave a job as a result of these responsibilities." One respondent "felt that he missed out on career advancement and made financial sacrifices to meet his parents' needs." Others indicated that caring for their older relatives while also raising children affected their romantic relationships. "I'll be honest," one respondent admitted. "It almost broke our marriage."[265]

Declining population could yield other negative societal effects too.

- **CULTURAL LOSS:** Indigenous communities have long experienced declining fertility and population. This amounts to an extinction event because they contain so few people to begin with. Thousands of indigenous cultures are already "in jeopardy of disappearing within developing countries," say Darrell Bricker and John Ibbitson in *Empty Planet*[266]—and their rich traditions along with them.

- **BLIGHT:** We already see this in places where groups have abandoned rural areas to seek new opportunities in urban ones. But even urban areas will begin to contract as populations decline. This results in declining local tax revenues that could leave these areas "filled with empty buildings and crumbling infrastructure," says population historian David Reher. Indeed, says Reher, "It is not difficult to imagine enclaves of rich, fiercely guarded pockets of well-being surrounded by large areas which look more like what we might see in some science-fiction movies."[267]

- **ETHNONATIONALISM:** Trent MacNamara of the *Atlantic* observes, "Already there are signs that local low fertility is becoming a folk issue in much the same way that global high fertility became one during the 'population bomb' decades of the late 20th century." As a result, says MacNamara, "In countries with the longest records of low fertility, new fears of race suicide are fueling well-known populist and ethnonationalist movements."[268] This trend has become evident in some Eastern European countries, as well as in the United States, where white supremacism is on the rise.

Perhaps worst of all, humankind's creative capacity for innovation could be diminished. "More people can generate more ideas," say Tupy and Pooley in *Superabundance*. "Even if only a small fraction of humans can generate a good idea, the number of good ideas will grow in proportion to population growth."[269] Flip that statement around, and you begin to see that the number of good ideas could flag in tandem with population decline. This could prove disastrous during a period when technical innovations to compensate for a diminishing workforce could mean the difference between our existence and our extinction.

CHAPTER 7

PROMOTING FERTILITY

It's kind of an extreme assumption to think that countries aren't going to think their way out of the problem [of low fertility] for the next 80 years.

—JOHN WILMOTH, DIRECTOR, UNITED NATIONS POPULATION DIVISION[270]

I n their book *Empty Planet*, Darrell Bricker and John Ibbitson write, "Population decline isn't a good thing or a bad thing. But it is a big thing."[271]

I'd rephrase that first sentence a bit—I see population decline as both a good thing *and* a bad thing. But their second sentence is spot-on. Population decline is a big thing. We must acknowledge this enormous and important shift and account for it as we look to and plan for the future.

Low fertility, aging populations, and population decline are turning the world upside down—literally. Before, a large base of working-age people supported a much smaller group of dependent older people. Demographers describe this societal structure as a "population pyramid." Today because of the rising median age and high OADR of nearly every advanced economy on earth (and plenty of emerging ones too), the population pyramid looks more like a spinning top. And as the global population starts to decline, that spinning top will morph into an arrowhead balancing on its tip.

How all this plays out in any given society will depend largely on how effectively that society has prepared for it. The trick is to develop a plan that capitalizes on the benefits associated with population decline (discussed in chapter 5) while mitigating the risks (covered in chapter 6). That's what the rest of this book is about—the different ways some countries have responded to population woes and other things we all might try.

ADDRESSING CHANGING DEMOGRAPHICS: A THREE-PRONGED APPROACH

Broadly speaking, there are three ways to address the issues associated with low fertility rates, aging societies, and population decline. One is to promote fertility, discussed in this chapter. Another is to tap into the talent of our older members of society (see chapter 8). The third is to draw in more immigrants (covered in chapter 9).

> **NOTE:** These actions don't exactly reflect the three main factors involved in calculating population projections—fertility rate, mortality rate, and immigration—but they do echo them.

Some of these actions will involve government policies. "Policies that countries pursue today can alter the trajectory for fertility, mortality, and migration,"[272] says the IHME. But I believe business can play a critical role too. For one thing, free markets and entrepreneurialism are the crucibles of innovation, something we'll need in the years to come. For another, business can support parents at work and encourage older employees to stay on board, which could help address our inevitable labor shortages. I'll talk about that in chapter 10.

> **NOTE:** My intention in the following chapters is not to advocate for any specific policy, program, or action. Rather, it's to lay out possible responses to an increasingly pressing problem.

WHERE ARE THE BABIES?

In the last three decades or so, more and more countries have recognized the dangers associated with falling fertility rates. A 2015 survey by the World Population Policies Database found that 28 percent of countries included increasing fertility among their national goals—up from 10 percent in 1976.[273] But how?

First, it's important to stress that it's not that people don't want to have babies. They absolutely do. Babies are adorable. And "Babies have always represented humanity's best, boldest, most beautiful infinite possibilities," says Wajahat Ali in a 2019 TED Talk.[274] Plus, having babies is a biological imperative. As a species, we are hardwired to want babies.

The problem, says the UNPD, is that "a number of factors—such as economic instability, insufficient childcare options, and the difficulty of reconciling work and family duties—prevent people from actually having the number of children they want."[275] According to a recent US study, younger women say they want to have 2.1 babies.[276] And yet the 2021 US fertility rate was just 1.66.[277]

It doesn't help that in many societies, mothers are seen as home-makers and caregivers, even when they have full-time jobs outside the home, while fathers … well, aren't. Women do almost twice as much domestic work and childcare as fathers, even though there are now more women than men in the workforce.[278] And working moms today spend almost as much time with their kids as stay-at-home moms did in 1965.[279] I suspect that when considering whether to start a family or have more children, this reality gives many women pause, especially those with career aspirations.

> **NOTE:** You start to see why more and more couples have dogs instead of kids. In the United States, there are now more dogs (seventy-eight million)[280] than there are kids under eighteen (seventy-four million)[281]!

Persuading people to have babies isn't so much about selling them on the concept of babies. It's about addressing the factors that keep people from having the number of babies they really want. This generally involves instituting family-friendly policies and perhaps even offering financial incentives to encourage couples to reproduce. But it's also about encouraging cultural changes that promote gender equity. These policies and changes are the focus of this chapter.

> **NOTE:** The fact that people say they want more kids than they actually have is good news because it means if we do a better job of supporting families, fertility could increase.

FAMILY-FRIENDLY GOVERNMENT POLICIES

One way to increase fertility rates is to institute family-friendly government policies. These include the obvious provisions—extended paid parental leave, childcare, and education. But they could also involve fuzzier initiatives, such as cultivating a family-friendly society. The idea is to create conditions in which young people feel confident that "they will be able to embark on family formation with tolerable levels of economic loss and acceptable impacts on individual aspirations," says demographer Peter McDonald.[282]

In McDonald's view, the state *should* enact these types of family-friendly policies because it's the state's fault we have low fertility in the first place. "In their support for or promotion of social liberalism and economic deregulation, often through legislation," says McDonald, "states have been principal players in the higher risks now associated with family life." (By *risks*, McDonald means less protection for workers and wages, less job security, a general lack of support for parents and families, and so on.)

So he says, "States must also be the principal players in restoring the social balance." This will require a "compensatory wave in which the state and other institutions provide a new and substantial priority to the support of family life—especially in the bearing and rearing of children."[283]

> **NOTE:** The same government programs designed to promote fertility can also have "massive positive side effects on individual well-being and the strength of economies and societies at large," says the UNFPA.[284]

PAID PARENTAL LEAVE

The benefits of paid parental leave upon the birth or adoption of a child are immeasurable. Paid parental leave "contributes to the children's healthy development, improves maternal health, supports fathers' involvement in care, and enhances families' economic security," say Kathleen Romig and Kathleen Bryant at the Center of Budget and Policy Priorities.[285] That's a win-win-win-win.

It might seem counterintuitive, but paid parental leave can benefit employers too. Paid leave "promotes employee retention, increases morale and productivity, and reduces absenteeism and staff turnover," say Barbara Janta and Katherine Stewart at RAND Corporation.[286] Studies also show that paid leave increases overall participation in the labor force, particularly for mothers, especially when paid leave policies are paired with policies to protect parents' jobs while they are away.[287]

Many acknowledge the importance of paid parental leave for mothers. But fathers need it too. Paid parental leave lets dads bond with their babies and develop important parental skills (think feeding the baby, changing the baby's diaper, putting the baby to bed, etc.). It improves gender equity at home and at work because it dismantles the notion that women are the "caregivers" and men are the "breadwinners."

GENDER EQUITY AT HOME AND AT WORK

Gender inequity is a main reason many women choose to have fewer children or none at all. "Considerably greater equality in the division of family and home responsibilities between men and women are more likely to lead to a sizable rebound in the U.S. fertility rate," say economists Melissa Kearney and Phillip Levine at the Aspen Institute.[288]

At work, promoting gender equity means implementing "non-gender specific workplace policies ... support of workers with family responsibilities irrespective of gender, removal of institutional remnants of the male breadwinner model of the family, acceptance of fathers as parents by service providers, and more general recognition and support to fathers as parents," says McDonald.[289]

At home, though, it really just falls to individual men to do "their fair share of household chores, childcare, transportation for children's activities, the emotional labor of planning and tracking activities, and supporting their partner's career," say David G. Smith and W. Brad Johnson at *Harvard Business Review*.[290]

Most advanced economies offer paid parental leave, though new mothers typically get more than new fathers. For example, in the European Union, mothers receive 14 weeks of paid parental leave, but fathers get just 10 days.

Some countries have more generous parental leave policies. Britain allows moms 39 weeks (although dads get just 2). In Japan, both moms and dads get 52 weeks. In Sweden, parents receive 480 days in total, which they may divide between them however they see fit. And in Estonia, mothers get 140 days, fathers get 2 weeks, and together they can split an additional 435 days.

The United States isn't so generous. In fact, it isn't generous at all. The United States is the only advanced economy with no national paid leave program. Zero. Some US states mandate paid parental leave, and some employers offer it voluntarily but nowhere near enough: just 23 percent of private sector workers have access to paid parental leave.[291] Worse, millions of Americans lack even *unpaid* leave! If the United States is serious about improving its fertility rate, it'll need to do better than that.

FREE OR SUBSIDIZED CHILDCARE AND EDUCATION

In addition to paid parental leave, "Providing widely available, accessible, and high-quality childcare … is indispensable to sustaining higher fertility rates," says the UNFPA.[292] The same goes for education. Really, if the aim is to increase fertility, then both childcare and education should be free or at least subsidized.

> **NOTE:** Offering quality education is important for another reason: it increases the likelihood that our next generations will have the skills and smarts to meet the challenges associated with population decline as they age.

TWO BIRDS/ONE STONE

In Italy, currently tied with Spain for the lowest fertility rate in Europe (1.28), a pilot project in Piacenza put a preschool inside a nursing home. This, they believe, effectively solves two problems at once: enriching the lives of the elderly residents while also occupying the children. Communities seeking ways to increase access to childcare could consider replicating projects like this one.

CULTIVATING A FAMILY-FRIENDLY ENVIRONMENT

Some experts believe that communities designed and built with kids and families in mind can stimulate fertility. "Child-friendly urban design may be a pro-natalist policy,"[293] says McDonald.

Designing (or redesigning) urban spaces to be more family-friendly might mean adding and enlarging pedestrian areas, constructing public recreational facilities such as playgrounds and ballparks, and promoting safe neighborhood practices. It could also entail locating childcare centers, schools, and even places of employment nearer to residential areas to enable couples to balance work and family responsibilities.

NOTE: Housing subsidies could offset high housing costs to help families afford homes near their work and school.

Beyond modifying public spaces, communities could encourage the formation of families by helping young adults form romantic bonds—for example, organizing singles events and outings and perhaps providing relationship education and counseling. Communities could even borrow from the government of South Korea's playbook, which calls for public buildings to shut off their lights at 7:30 p.m. on the third Wednesday of each month to entice workers to go home early and spend time with (or start a) family.[294]

> **NOTE:** One thing that doesn't promote fertility? Calling people without kids "selfish," like Japanese lawmaker Toshihiro Nikai did in 2018!

FINANCIAL INCENTIVES TO INCREASE FERTILITY

In the United States, kids are extremely expensive, from the moment they're born—literally. Peterson-Kaiser Family Foundation estimates that delivering a baby costs $18,865 on average. If you have insurance, at least some of that bill will be covered. If not ... well, you do the math.

From there, the cost of kids climbs. As noted in chapter 2, in 2018 the median annual cost of childcare in the United States ranged from $4,801 to $15,417 ($5,357 to $17,171 in 2022 dollars).[295] That's for one child. Try adding two or more into the mix! For many prospective parents, having a family isn't financially feasible unless mom or dad quits their job to care for the kids at home, in which case they *still* take a serious economic hit because they lose one paycheck.

> **NOTE:** The rest of us take a hit when this happens too because we all lose one capable worker. This might not seem like such a big deal now, but it will be as our societies age and our labor pool contracts.

Ultimately, according to the US Department of Agriculture, raising a child through age seventeen costs middle-income, married-couple parents $233,610. That number covers food, shelter, and other necessities until that child reaches adulthood.[296] But it's not like the costs associated with raising kids stop there. For many families, there are college costs, which in the United States are *bonkers*. Recall from chapter 2 that since 1970 the average cost for tuition, room, and board at a four-year state college has ballooned from $1,238 per year ($9,338 in 2023 dollars) to $21,337 today[297] and that private schools cost even more. And yet median income hasn't kept up. In 1970 the median income was $9,870. That's $78,861 in 2023 dollars. But the actual median income at the time of this writing (January 2023) is $68,703.

> **NOTE:** Expensive health insurance in some countries greatly adds to the cost of raising children.

Add all that together—birth and food and shelter and necessities and college—and you're looking at hundreds of thousands of dollars. That's like buying a house! Except "You can't sell your children, they never appreciate in value," Jonathan V. Last dryly observes in *What to Expect When No One's Expecting*. "And there's a good chance that, somewhere around age 16, they'll announce: 'I hate you.'"[298]

Many countries with very low fertility have begun paying couples to have kids. The idea is to "reduce the personal cost to parents of having or raising children," say Kearney and Levine.[299] Some of these financial incentives are tax breaks—credits, deductions, or rebates. Others are loans, issued to couples who marry and forgiven after they have a set number of children. Some countries even dole out cash—baby bonuses bequeathed right after delivery or periodically until the child reaches a certain age.

This is happening in China, where, in the face of a shrinking population, government officials now issue "tax and housing credits, educational benefits and even cash incentives to encourage women to have more children," says Alexandra Stevenson in the *New York Times*.[300] Japan, whose population has dropped every year since 2007, offers similar incentives. And in South Korea, the government distributes what it calls "parent pay"—a 1 million won ($740) monthly stipend for one year after the birth of a baby and half that amount for a second year.[301]

Financial incentives are particularly popular in Eastern Europe. This is particularly true in Hungary, where the government, led by ultraright-wing prime minister Viktor Orbán, issues zero-interest loans of up to 10 million forints ($25,410) to young married couples, which the government then forgives for couples who produce three or more children.[302]

But that's not all. In December 2022 Orbán tweeted, "Women who become mothers before turning 30 will be exempt from paying personal tax!" According to Jessica Grose at the *New York Times*, "That's on top of a raft of other initiatives meant to boost the number of Hungarian babies, including allowing mothers of four or more children to be permanently exempt from paying taxes, a mortgage repayment plan for families with two or more children," etc.[303]

For Orbán, these initiatives aren't just about boosting Hungary's fertility rate. They're about ensuring Hungary's ethnic purity. Orbán recently went as far as to warn Hungarians against race mixing with non-Europeans, insisting, "We [Hungarians] are not a mixed race ... and we do not want to become a mixed race."[304] Yikes.

Russian president Vladimir Putin is said to be "obsessed" with raising fertility. "In his mind, the power of a country is linked to the size of its population," says demographer Laurent Chalard.[305] Putin recently revived the Soviet-era honorific "Mother Heroine" for women who bear ten children—a title that also includes a one-time payment of 1 million rubles ($16,120) on the tenth child's first birthday, *if* all ten children survive (or die in service to the country).[306] But even that won't be enough to boost Russia anywhere near the replacement rate or restore its flagging population numbers. Indeed, some experts suggest this could be one reason Putin ordered the invasion of Ukraine in February 2022. By absorbing Ukraine's population, Russia's would immediately grow by some forty-three million people.

NOTE: Apart from government incentives, a robust economy can help promote fertility because more young couples have confidence in their ability to thrive within that economy. Conversely, "During economic crises, people are less inclined to have children," says Russian demographer Alexey Raksha.[307]

BABY BONUSES AND BACHELOR TAXES

Financial incentives to promote fertility aren't new. In ancient Sparta, fathers with three sons were spared military duty, and fathers with four sons paid zero taxes. In ancient Rome, married people with children received special perks, such as better seats at the theater.

On a related note, to urge single men to marry and start a family, Caesar Augustus imposed a bachelor tax. Bachelor taxes were also levied by the French during World War I and by Mussolini during the 1920s. And communist leaders in the Soviet Union issued lump sum payments for new babies, housing bonuses, and work allowances. "None of these attempts was successful," says Last.[308]

DO PRONATALIST POLICIES WORK?

The short answer to this question is, not really. But sometimes, when the right policies are applied to the right environment, and in the right combination, some progress can be made.

NOTE: There is no single one-size-fits-all policy guaranteed to address fertility decline.

To quote Bloomberg columnist Gearoid Reidy, who himself borrowed from Leo Tolstoy, "All fertile societies are alike; each infertile society is infertile in its own way."[309] So societies with very low fertility must determine *why* they are infertile. Only then will they be able to identify and implement an appropriate assemblage policies to reverse or at least halt declining fertility rates.

> **NOTE:** Even if countries do everything right, their chances of restoring fertility rates to replacement levels are minimal, especially countries with very low fertility.

Notice my use of the word *assemblage*. Taken on its own, no single pronatalist policy can move the fertility needle much. However, "Fertility rates can recover from very low levels and populations can grow when certain elements are in place," says the UNFPA.[310] These generally include the government policies discussed in this chapter, such as parental leave (for both parents), gender equity at work and at home, affordable childcare and education, financial incentives, and a robust economy. (Affordable housing and cost of living don't hurt either.)

Ultimately, though, says demographer Jan Hoem, "National fertility is possibly best seen as a systemic outcome that depends more on broader attributes, such as the degree of family-friendliness of a society, and less on the presence and detailed construction of monetary benefits."[311] This helps explain why even with all its government benefits, Hungary has raised its fertility rate from 1.2 to just 1.5—nowhere near the replacement rate.[312]

> **NOTE:** With these types of policies, continuity over a period of years is key. This gives the policies time to take root and reassures people that they're here to stay.

In the end, no government policy can persuade someone who does not want a baby to have one. "It seems to me that no amount of additional financial support would make a person want to be a parent without an intrinsic desire for children," observes Grose.[313] However, for people who *do* want children, these types of policies can help them fulfill their fertility desires. This is significant because as noted, lots of people say they want more children than they end up having.

ARTIFICIAL WOMBS

As technology progresses, tools to promote fertility—or more precisely to increase births—could take a new (if dystopian) form: artificial wombs.

Scientists are already developing artificial wombs to support *ex vivo gestation*—the gestation of a fetus outside the body of its mother. Their purpose is to support continued gestation for infants born extremely prematurely (before twenty-eight weeks) by simulating the conditions inside the mother's womb. This not only increases the baby's chances of survival, but it may also prevent the lifelong health problems that plague many preemies, such as cerebral palsy, vision and hearing issues, learning disabilities, and developmental delays.

Ultimately, though, artificial wombs *could* be used to gestate a fetus from in vitro fertilization to delivery—a process called *complete ectogenesis*. As creepy as it sounds, complete ecto-genesis could have some positive applications. For example, it could be used by women who cannot become pregnant or who are unable to or don't want to carry a fetus to term. It also opens doors for nonbinary and transgender people who want children. And freeing women from what 1970s feminist Shulamith Firestone famously called the "tyranny of reproduction" might improve gender equality.[314]

But there are some practical and ethical issues associated with artificial wombs. Like, could a pregnant woman seeking an abortion be forced to place her fetus in an artificial womb instead? Could eugenicists use artificial wombs to grow "designer babies" in labs, preselecting their intelligence, complexion, hair color, eye color, height, and body type? What is the legal status of the fetus in the artificial womb? It's been removed from the mother, so is it *completely* born? Or just *kind of* born? And what do you call it? A fetus? A baby? Or something else, like *gestateling* or *fetonate*, as some scientists have suggested? Then there's the issue of expense. At least at first, artificial wombs and their use will be prohibitively expensive. Will only preemies from rich families have access to them? That seems wrong.

For now these questions are moot. Using artificial wombs to support ex vivo gestation has not yet been tested for humans (but artificial wombs have been used to grow lambs). And although scientists believe current artificial womb technology *could* support ex vivo gestation for humans, it can't yet do it "from scratch." In the future, however, "It is not unreasonable that we might have the capacity to develop a human embryo from fertilization to birth entirely outside the uterus," says developmental biologist Dr. Paul Tesar.[315]

THE DOWNSIDES OF PRONATALIST POLICIES

Policies to promote fertility (which also boost quality of life more generally) sound great—and they can be. But they cost a lot. And when I say a lot, I mean *a lot*.

President Orbán of Hungary earmarked roughly 5 percent of that country's GDP to cover financial incentives for young married couples to have kids.[316] That's three times what the country spends on its military.[317] Putin's program in Russia costs an estimated 400 billion rubles ($6.532 billion) per year.[318] South Korea has spent hundreds of billions of dollars to reverse declining fertility with underwhelming results.[319] Between 1990 and 2015, Japan quadrupled its spending on family-friendly policies only to see fertility go *down*.[320]

There are indirect costs too. According to the UNPD, "Cash benefits tend to drive women out of the workforce"—the opposite of what they're meant to do. "This means lower tax revenues, and higher numbers of women dependent on social transfers."[321]

Some pronatalist policies veer into something darker: an attempt by the state to control population size through coercion. For example, "Some countries have in the past sought to increase the total fertility rate by restricting access to reproductive health services," say IHME researchers.[322] As one example, Romanian dictator Nicolae Ceaușescu outlawed contraception and abortion (with few exceptions), required government-enforced gynecological exams, described giving birth as "a patriotic duty," and considered fetuses "the socialist property of the entire society."[323] Today, says the IHME, "A very real danger exists that, in the face of declining population, some places might consider adopting policies that restrict female reproductive health rights and access to services."[324]

This cannot happen. "Whatever the demographic situation of a country, it cannot justify population policies that undermine basic human rights," says Michael Hermann, a senior advisor at the UNFPA. Instead, population policies must "focus on empowering people to achieve their reproductive aspirations through the realization of sexual and reproductive health and rights, and support rather than undermine fundamental human rights more broadly."[325] In other words, say Christian Shepherd and Lyric Li of the *Washington Post*, "While having a child should be everyone's right, it isn't anyone's responsibility."[326]

THE CASE FOR ADAPTATION

Taking some or all of the steps described in this chapter could improve fertility rates. But it is unlikely that countries currently contending with low fertility will ever reach replacement rates again, at least not in this century. The math just isn't there.

Instead of promoting fertility, it might make more sense to adapt to a new, low-fertility reality. "Countries need to consider and plan for future demographic changes and build institutions and societies that are resilient to and can thrive amid these demographic changes," says Hermann.[327]

Adapting to low fertility might also mean "invest[ing] more in the people we've already got—both children and their parents—so everyone becomes a productive and capable adult," suggests Stephanie H. Murray at FiveThirtyEight.[328] That way, she says, "The next generation of workers may constitute a smaller slice of

Instead of promoting fertility, it might make more sense to adapt to a new, low-fertility reality.

the population, but they'll be more educated and thus more produc-tive and better poised to satisfy the needs of older people."[329]

Ultimately, says the UNFPA, what's important isn't so much "the number of people in a country." It's "a population's combined human capital, irrespective of population size."[330] We'll talk more about that in the chapters to come.

CHAPTER 8

TAPPING THE TALENT OF OUR ELDERS

If I have seen further it is by standing
on the shoulders of giants.

—SIR ISAAC NEWTON, SCIENTIST

We've talked a lot about problems associated with aging societies. Having too few workers, producing too few goods and services, results in decreased productivity, lower profit margins, higher prices, reduced demand for consumer goods, rising inflation, rising interest rates, reduced risk capital for entrepreneurs, decreased growth (or none at all), the collapse of popular social services such as national health insurance and social security programs, governments defaulting on debt … you get the idea. This silver tsunami threatens to swamp societies around the globe.

But what do we mean when we say *aging societies*? Who are we talking about?

The most common answer to this question is anyone over age sixty-five. That's the number most social scientists use to calculate a population's OADR, which compares the number of old people (dependents) in a given population with the number of young people (producers). This makes sense because most of us consider sixty-five*ish* to be retirement age.

If we want to head off the problems associated with an aging population ... then we need to tap into the talent of our elders.

Here's what *doesn't* make sense: the notion of people over sixty-five as *dependents*, not *producers*. We all know plenty of people who remain fit and vibrant well into their seventies, eighties, and even nineties. Do we really want to relegate members of this group—who have vast experience in life and work, who possess deep wisdom, who are plenty capable of producing, and from whom we all have much to learn—to the status of *dependent*? No. This group is an incredible resource and should be treated as such.

NOTE: Economists Charles Goodhart and Manoj Pradhan define the word "dependency" differently in terms of health ("being in need of outside care and assistance") than in a macroeconomic context (relating to "certain specific age groups, irrespective of their physical condition").[331] But I see these definitions converging because of the ever-increasing prevalence of ageism. I'll talk more about ageism shortly.

If we want to head off the problems associated with an aging population—if we want to ride the silver tsunami instead of drowning in it—then we need to tap into the talent of our elders. We must redefine and perhaps even recalculate "old age." We must adopt a new approach to aging, both as a society and as individuals, one in which we remain as healthy, vital, and engaged as possible, for as long as possible. That's the topic of this chapter.

EARLY ATTITUDES TOWARD THE ELDERLY

We didn't always put our elders out to pasture when they reached a certain age. In most societies they remained esteemed members of their clan or community, producing food, performing skilled labor such as forging tools or weapons or weaving baskets or textiles, caring for grandchildren, and so on.

Most importantly, older people were "repositories of information," says scientist and author Jared Diamond. According to Diamond, the knowledge retained by a society's elders often meant "the difference between survival and death for their whole society in a time of crisis caused by rare events for which only the oldest people alive [had] experience."[332]

> **NOTE:** Admittedly, not all early societies granted their older members such high status. Some nomadic groups neglected, abandoned, or even killed elders whose usefulness or physical capacity expired.

In traditional Asian cultures, elders weren't just respected; they were revered. This attitude, called *xiao* (meaning *filial piety*), called for obedience, deference, devotion, and service to one's elders, especially parents and older family members. First articulated by Confucius during the Chou Dynasty, xiao became a foundational principle of Chinese society and morality. Even today the Chinese adhere to xiao, although doing so has become increasingly difficult for practical reasons because of China's rapid industrialization and urbanization and its relative dearth of young people.

Over time xiao spread from China to Korea (*hyo*) to Japan (*kō*). But these countries weren't the only ones to venerate their elders. In India, both in the past and today, the elderly are "generally obeyed, revered, considered to be fountains of knowledge and wisdom, and treated with respect and dignity by family and community members," writes Indian professor Dr. N. K. Chadha.[333]

As for the West, "The ancient Greeks generally abhorred aging as it represented a decline from highly prized youth and vigor," writes Dr. Mark E. Williams. "However, older warriors, elder philosophers and statesmen were typically well-treated."[334] The ancient Romans maintained a similar stance.

The proliferation of Christianity softened Western views on the aged. Various Bible passages instruct Christians to honor their elders, like "You who are younger, be subject to the elders" (1 Pet. 5:5, English Standard Version), "Gray hair is a crown of glory; it is gained in a righteous life" (Prov. 16:31, ESV), and "Honour thy father and thy mother" (Exod. 20:12, King James Version). And of course, the Christian god is generally depicted as an elderly man.

THE AGE OF AGEISM

Before the 1700s, "Anglo-American culture generally prescribed 'veneration' as the proper attitude of youth toward age," says gerontologist and historian Thomas R. Cole. Moreover, "Acknowledgment of the intractable sorrows and infirmities of old age remained culturally acceptable."[335]

Eventually, though, cultural shifts altered these attitudes. One such shift was the growing emphasis on work due to the ascendance of the so-called "Protestant work ethic." This work ethic "ties an individual's value to his or her ability to work—something that diminishes in old age,"[336] observes journalist Karina Martinez-Carter. Another shift, at least in the United States, was "our American emphasis on the virtues of self-reliance," says Diamond. "We instinctively look down on older people who are no longer self-reliant and independent."[337] Beyond that, say researchers at the US National Academies of Sciences, Engineering, and Medicine (commonly referred to as simply the *National Academies*), the following developments helped alter attitudes about the elderly:

> (1) Widespread literacy and mass media replaced a reliance on elders' wisdom; (2) industrialization required nimble adaptation to changeable modern skill sets, rather than traditional practices; (3) families became more nuclear and had less need for multigenerational contributions.[338]

By the early 1900s, older members of Western societies were no longer seen as valuable "repositories of information." Rather, they were viewed as a drag on society—"dependent, in need of services, and incapable of leading 'real' lives," writes Cole.[339]

Renowned psychiatrist Dr. Robert Butler coined a term for this view: *ageism*. Butler described ageism as prejudice against old people, often expressed through "stereotypes and myths, outright disdain and dislike, or simply subtle avoidance of contact; discriminatory practices in housing, employment and services of all kinds; epithets, cartoons and jokes."[340]

Today ageism pervades most Western societies—and increasingly, some Eastern ones too. According to the National Academies, "Across a variety of countries, older people are universally viewed as well-intentioned but incompetent, 'doddering but dear.'"[341] Frankly, that's putting it nicely. More often, older people are described as "conservative, unproductive, disengaged, inflexible, serene, poor, sick, or in a nursing home," says Cole.[342] Or, in the vernacular of both macroeconomics *and* healthcare, they're *dependents*.

> **NOTE:** Many elderly people absorb and even perpetuate ageist views. As a result, says Harvard psychology professor Ellen Langer, they display "decreased effort, less use of adaptive strategies, avoidance of challenging situations, and failure to seek medical attention for disease-related symptoms."[343]

THE "NEW OLD"

Old age as we perceive it is just that: a perception. There's no *empirical* definition of old age. "In societal and scientific discourse, aging is usually assumed to present a phenomenon taking place during a specific phase or stage of life, with specific characteristics," says philosopher Hanne Laceulle. But "the starting point of the phase or stage of aging is rather obscure and arbitrarily coupled to a certain chronological age, for example 65 or 70."[344]

Complicating matters, the number with which old age is "arbitrarily coupled" is subject to change. In earlier eras, old age might have been forty, fifty, or perhaps sixty years. Yes, some people enjoyed lengthier lives, but that just meant they were thought of as old for that much longer. And of course, now we say sixty-five is old age—or at least, retirement age.

If the numerical value that constitutes old age is not set in stone, then why do we act like it is? If someone is still vital, if they're still engaged, passionate, and sharp, why should their numerical age matter? Is it right to assume that simply because of someone's numerical age, they have nothing left to contribute? How is that good for them? How is that good for any of us?

There are, of course, certain things that become more difficult for some people as they grow older. But Diamond observes, "There are other things that [older people] can do better than younger people." The challenge for society, he says, "is to make use of those things that older people are better at doing."[345]

So what are those things? Diamond cites a few examples: "supervising, administering, advising, strategizing, teaching, synthesizing, and devising long-term plans."[346] More than that, he says older people offer "experience, understanding of people and human relationships, ability to help other people without [their] own ego getting in the way, and interdisciplinary thinking."[347]

Many of these boil down to one single quality: wisdom. Psychologists Paul B. Baltes and Ursula M. Staudinger of the Max Planck Institute for Human Development define *wisdom* as "an expertise in the conduct and meaning of life."[348] In recent years we've devalued—ignored, even—the importance of wisdom. Now data is king. Don't get me wrong, data is great for solving tons of problems. But when faced with difficulties on a monumental scale—things such as wars, pandemics, and economic depressions—wisdom is what we need. Older people have it. Younger people don't.

NOTE: Unfortunately, observes Dr. Philip Pizzo, former dean of the Stanford University School of Medicine, "We have not reached the point where respect for wisdom is valued as much as respect of perceived vigor of performance."[349] At least, not yet.

Speaking of younger people, often, when people talk about redefining old age, what they *really* mean is finding ways to stay young. This is not what I'm talking about. Attempting to stay young, says the WHO, simply causes us to "feel shame about getting older and limit what [we] think [we] can do, instead of taking pride in the accomplishment of aging."[350] What I *am* talking about is something psychiatrists call *conscious aging*. Conscious aging is a "way of looking at and experiencing aging that moves beyond our cultural obsession with youth toward a respect and need for the wisdom of age," says Dr. Stephan Rechtschaffen.[351] Conscious aging means dismissing the prevailing view that old age is an incurable disease and instead acknowledging and even embracing what it actually is: a natural and meaningful part of our life cycle.

Shifting our views on aging will benefit older people, of course. But it will help younger people too. At present, "We have no role models for growing old gracefully, only for postponing it,"[352] Dartmouth professor Jere Daniel observes. So psychoanalyst Erik Erikson says, "Lacking a culturally viable ideal of old age, our civilization does not really harbor a concept of the whole life."[353] This must change.

DELAYING RETIREMENT

We've established that sixty-five is generally considered to be retirement age. But have you ever wondered why?

Well, it wasn't always. In fact, retirement at any age wasn't really a "thing" until the late 1800s. Before that time, says Stephen Mihm at Bloomberg, companies "kept graying workers on the payroll"—in some cases "out of compassion" and in others because older employees were "more conservative and consequently less likely to succumb to radicalism and strikes." But as progressive reformers and labor activists began agitating for shorter workdays and a five-day workweek, companies "needed to produce the same amount as before, but with far fewer hours," says Mihm.[354] So believing that productivity declined with age, most employers targeted older workers for dismissal.

It was in this context that conservative German chancellor Otto von Bismarck, under pressure from socialist opponents, rolled out the first-ever national social security program in 1889. "Those who are disabled from work by age and invalidity have a well-grounded claim to care from the state," Bismarck argued before the Reichstag.[355] Bismarck set the retirement age at seventy for one simple reason: few German workers lived that long. In 1916, however, due again to efforts by progressive reformers and labor activists, the German government reduced the age of eligibility to sixty-five.

In 1935 the US Congress enacted the Social Security Act as part of Franklin D. Roosevelt's New Deal. The Social Security Act, modeled after Germany's social security program, provided retirement benefits for American workers over age sixty-five. But as in Bismarck's Germany, relatively few American workers ever became eligible for social security benefits because the average life expectancy for American men in 1935 was just fifty-eight years.[356]

NOTE: While the Social Security Act was intended to bolster the fortunes of older Americans, it had another objective too: to remove them from the labor force to make room for younger workers. That might have been a good idea then, but now, not so much.

The average human life span has soared since the days of Bismarck and Roosevelt. In the United States, the average life span is a tick over seventy-nine years.[357] Moreover, in 2021 Americans who reached age sixty-five could expect to live an additional eighteen-plus years on average.[358] Further advances in science and medicine could soon add thirty (or more!) healthy years to the human life span.

NOTE: The average life span in the United States is nowhere near the longest. Both Hong Kong and Japan boast average life spans of more than eighty-five years.[359]

Despite this, the average retirement age, which generally coincides with eligibility for government benefits such as social security, has remained effectively the same. In fact, it's slightly lower. In 2020 among the thirty-eight member states of the Organisation for Economic Co-operation and Development, the average retirement age was 64.2 years for men and 63.4 years for women.[360] If general trends in average life span continue, these retirees could be "dependents," receiving retirement benefits such as social security, for decades to come. This is not sustainable.

THE EFFECTS OF COVID-19 ON RETIREMENT TRENDS

Millions of Americans lost their jobs during the COVID-19 pandemic. But once vaccines became available and "normal" life resumed, most people returned to work. The key word here: *most*. As recently as November 2022, the US labor force was still down roughly 3.5 million workers—a shortfall Federal Reserve Chair Jerome H. Powell attributed largely to "retirements in excess of what would have been expected from population aging alone."[361] Great Britain has experienced a similar trend. According to data from the British Office for National Statistics, the country now has nearly half a million more "economically inactive" working-aged people than in February 2020—nearly two-thirds of whom are over the age of fifty.[362] This glut of retirees is one largely underreported effect of COVID-19.

Programs such as social security, on which many older people rely for survival, are a little like Ponzi schemes: those at the bottom of the population pyramid (producers, or younger people) pay for those at the top (dependents, or older people). This worked fine when producers greatly outnumbered dependents, like in 1940, when the United States boasted roughly 42 producers for each dependent.[363] By 2021, however, we had just 2.8 producers per dependent, and the number will only fall from there.[364] You start to see how in 2021 the total cost of social security exceeded its total income by $56 billion.[365] In fact, the program's trustees predict that "total cost will exceed total income *in all future years*" (emphasis mine). In other words, social security will never again pull in more money than it puts out. There's no avoiding it: in an aging society, the math just doesn't work.

> **NOTE:** That's just social security. Medicare is a whole other thing where the math doesn't work.

Here in the United States, ensuring the solvency of our social security program requires some type of adjustment: pay more in, pay less out, pay out later, or some combination of the three. Paying more in and paying less out are topics for another forum. Here, I want to talk about paying out later—that is, delaying retirement.

> **NOTE:** In 1982 the US Congress amended the Social Security Act to gradually raise the age at which individuals become eligible for full social security benefits from sixty-five to sixty-seven. It's a move in the right direction, but life expectancies being what they are, it likely won't be enough.

Delaying retirement could help sustain government services such as social security. It could also significantly offset the coming workforce contraction. But most importantly, delaying retirement would allow us to tap into the talent and wisdom, the "repositories of knowledge," of our older workers. That's good for all of us.

Depending on what type of job they have, delaying retirement can be good for seniors too. For example, the National Academies says work can improve health "by promoting physical, cognitive, and social engagement."[366] And for people who really love their job, whose profession is part of their identity, delaying retirement helps them sustain their sense of purpose and self-esteem. Delaying retirement can even benefit people who might not *love* their job but enjoy the camaraderie they experience at work. This is significant when you consider that nearly one in five adults in the United States between the ages of sixty-two and ninety-one report frequent loneliness[367] and that loneliness can increase our risk of heart disease, stroke, depression, anxiety, dementia, and death.[368]

> **Delaying retirement would allow us to tap into the talent and wisdom, the "repositories of knowledge," of our older workers.**

> **NOTE:** Many older people continue working to keep their independence and retain meaning in their lives.

Putting off retirement has financial rewards too. After all, continuing to work means continuing to earn an income. This, say the National Academies, "has a larger impact on a household's standard of living than saving throughout the life course, particularly when individuals do not begin saving until they are middle-aged or older."[369]

In the United States, delaying retirement can also allow older workers to defer the collection of social security benefits. This offers a sizable pecuniary upside: "For each year beyond your full retirement age that you delay collecting social security benefits up to a maximum of age 70," explains Dave Bernard at *U.S. News & World Report*, "you will receive an additional 8 percent."[370]

Finally, Bernard observes that by delaying retirement, you "delay the time when you will become 100 percent responsible for your own health insurance premiums [assuming] your employer is picking up part of the tab." This can be the difference between "just making it" after retirement and "making it memorable," says Bernard.[371]

> **NOTE:** Raising the retirement age improves employment prospects for workers in their fifties because employers no longer see them as nearing retirement age.

I get it. For some people, delaying retirement is a hard sell. When French president Emmanuel Macron announced plans to raise France's retirement age from sixty-two to sixty-four in January 2023, more than a million protesters swarmed the streets in Paris. (Incidentally, this happened on a Thursday, otherwise known as a "workday.") "Retirement is considered sacred," Luc Rouban, a researcher in Paris, told the *New York Times*. "For many, it's like reaching paradise."[372]

Many older workers in the United States, where the retirement age is a grizzled sixty-seven, hold similar views. This is particularly true for workers who say they have "bad jobs," which, according to one 2019 survey, amounts to 50 percent of the US labor force.[373] These workers, along with workers whose jobs are physically demanding, are itching to retire as soon as humanly possible, and having to put it off, even for just a few years, can be a bitter pill to swallow.

Delaying retirement could also be considered unfair to the poorest among us because their average life span is shorter than that of more affluent members of society. According to a 2016 study published in the *Journal of American Medicine*, American men whose income is in the top 1 percent live fifteen years longer than those in the bottom 1 percent.[374] If everyone retires at the same age, rich and poor alike, then the rich will have much more time to enjoy their golden years than the poor will. So that's not great.

These are undoubtedly problems that need solving. But none of them negate the mathematical realities that call for delayed retirement.

NOTE: Chapter 10 talks more about how businesses might adapt to draw in more older workers.

NONPAYING WORK

Of course, you don't need to have a paying job to be a "producer." As retired dermatologist Stephanie Munn recently told the *New York Times*, "People can be contributing to the economy in another ways."[375]

Some older people might opt to do the "host of family, community, and social activities once performed by house-wives," says Fred Pearce in *The Coming Population Crash*.[376] As any stay-at-home parent will tell you, these activities, which could include childcare and household tasks, are as much "work" as anything else! Moreover, performing these types of activities frees up younger family members to seek employment outside the home.

Older people can also contribute by volunteering—for example, at a nonprofit organization. This not only helps these organizations do important work, but it can also "expand and strengthen social ties, while also bolstering various dimensions of health" for the older volunteer, says the National Academies.[377]

Finally, older people make great mentors . "Seniors are particularly suited to make unique contributions," says the nonprofit Positive Maturity. "They have plenty of wisdom and experience to share." Through mentoring, they say, "Older adults can derive fulfillment as well as a sense of value and purpose."[378]

IMPROVING AND PROMOTING HEALTH

If we want our older colleagues to stick around in the workplace, we must ensure that poor health does not prevent them from doing so. To quote the National Academies,

> Poor health can limit work opportunities by reducing an individual's physical, cognitive, or mental capacity for engaging in work activities, and also by altering preferences for job characteristics, remaining in the labor force, and the type of work in which to engage.[379]

Fortunately, the latter decades of the twentieth century brought dramatic improvements in human health because of rapid advances in both medicine and public health practices. As a result, millions of people extended not only their life span but also their *health span*—"the amount of time that people spend healthy and active, with a good quality of life," explains Dr. Daniela J. Lamas.[380] And they compressed morbidity, meaning they remained vital and largely free of disease and disability until just before death.[381]

More recently, however, these upward trends have tilted downward, at least in the United States. For lots of reasons—including substance abuse, obesity, suicide, and COVID-19—working-age adults in the United States have begun dying in higher numbers. This disturbing development suggests that the next cohort of older workers is less healthy than the current one, which could prevent them from working as long as is needed.

> **NOTE:** Many older workers, particularly women, stop working to care for family members who fall ill—another negative impact of poor public health on the labor force.

Ensuring we have enough healthy senior employees now and in the future requires investment in the life sciences, especially in research into afflictions associated with aging, and in gerontechnology, or elder tech (technology geared toward a geriatric population).

These types of investments will do more than just promote and improve health and well-being. They could yield other benefits too. For example, when older people stay healthy, they remain independent for longer, which decreases the burden on healthcare and other caregiving systems. This could be critical in the coming years as the number of older people grows and the labor force (including the number of healthcare workers) contracts.

> **NOTE:** Although we will have more old people to care for in the coming years, we'll also have fewer children to look after. This could help mitigate workforce shortages.

LIFE SCIENCES

Several health conditions often accompany old age. I put these conditions in two categories: non-life-threatening infirmities that affect otherwise healthy adults, such as hearing loss, vision loss, osteoarthritis, and so on, and life-threatening illnesses such as diabetes, heart disease, pulmonary disease, cancer, and the like. All these conditions, and countless more, can diminish a person's quality of life and ability to remain independent, let alone employed. Clearly, eradicating them would be a game changer.

Many older adults also suffer from age-related mental conditions—most notably dementia, often caused by Alzheimer's disease. The horrors associated with dementia are obvious: the loss of one's memory, one's capabilities, and one's dignity. But apart from these, there's also the fact that dementia does not curtail the human life span. Instead, observe Goodhart and Pradhan, "It incapacitates those who are afflicted and therefore involves a large use of resources to care for them."[382] Many of these resources are human caregivers, which, as mentioned, could become scarce in years to come. More than 55 million people worldwide currently suffer from dementia; by 2050 that number is predicted to spike to 139 million.[383] Finding a cure for this devastating condition is crucial, and yet, say Goodhart and Pradhan, "the amounts devoted to research are tiny."[384] This is a problem we must solve.

RETHINKING END-OF-LIFE DECISIONS

As we age, many of us suffer from painful and debilitating medical conditions or contract terminal illnesses that cause great misery and diminish our quality of life.

Recent years have seen a growing movement in support of *euthanasia*—killing or permitting the painless death of a hopelessly sick or injured person as an act of mercy—to allow people to end their suffering. Since then, a handful of countries and US states have enacted laws to permit this practice in some form or another (though in most cases with significant requirements and restrictions).

Euthanasia is *extremely* controversial. Proponents view the ability to "die with dignity" as a basic human right, while opponents contend that it devalues human life. Remarks made by Yale professor Yusuke Narita in 2021—who called for "mass suicide and mass 'seppuku' [suicide by disembowelment] of the elderly"[385]—have not helped matters. (Yusuke later claimed he was speaking metaphorically. Let's hope so.)

I'm not here to make a case one way or another. But it's relevant here because many societies invest significant resources in keeping suffering people alive. As the effects of aging populations continue to manifest, finding common ground on the subject of euthanasia will become more urgent.

GERONTECHNOLOGY

As populations around the world have aged, innovative companies have begun developing technologies geared toward older people. These *gerontechnologies*, as they're called, could help our elders maintain their health and remain vibrant, engaged, and perhaps even employed. More importantly, they can enable more seniors to age in place (at home) rather than in elder care facilities. In addition to improving the quality of life of older members of society, such a development would also reduce the burden on straining healthcare systems and the need for human caregivers.

> **NOTE:** An obvious example of an effective gerontechnology is telemedicine. Its utility became even more evident during the COVID-19 pandemic.

In recent years start-up companies and existing firms have developed all manner of elder tech gadgets. Many of these are relatively simple in concept—mobile phone apps or automatic pill dispensers to remind seniors to take their medication, devices that detect when someone falls and notify a caregiver, and panic buttons to call for help when needed. Some address mobility issues, such as smart walkers with electric motors, sensors, and automatic acceleration and braking to navigate slopes and uneven surfaces and smart wheelchairs that detect obstacles. Others act as helpers, such as assistive robots that perform simple household tasks such as vacuuming or handling laundry.

NOTE: Healthcare technology tools also act as a "force multiplier" in healthcare organizations, enabling them "to deliver excellent care with fewer nurses and other providers," writes nurse futurist Bonnie Clipper.[386] This will become critical as the number of available healthcare providers shrinks.

Recently, researchers at companies such as IBM have begun connecting elder tech devices to the Internet of Things to enable family members, doctors, and other caregivers to monitor the well-being of older people still living at home. These include cameras; wearable gadgets that monitor a person's vital signs or detect falls; pressure sensors in a bed that detect whether it is occupied; sensors that track when lights are turned on or off, doors are opened or closed, appliances (such as toasters or teakettles) are powered up, or toilets are flushed; and so on. AI and machine learning tools analyze data from these devices for unusual patterns—for example, if a person is still in bed past their usual time or hasn't turned on the kettle when they normally do—and send a text notification or email message to a family member or other caregiver in the event of an anomaly.

NOTE: Nontechnological home modifications promote aging in place, too—things such as brighter lighting, handrails, ramps, and lifts.

APPLYING PUBLIC POLICIES TO PROMOTE WORK AND ENCOURAGE AGING IN PLACE

A variety of public policies are designed to address the issues flagged in this chapter, including policies to promote the continued participation of older workers in the labor force and to encourage aging in place.

The most obvious policies to promote the continued participation of older workers in the labor force are those that delay the provision of social security and similar benefits and those that reward older workers who stay on the job. In addition to these, "a host of other policies, addressing retirement savings, paid and unpaid leave to address caregiving responsibilities, subsidies to provide formal care, and retraining may also improve financial resources or opportunities to continue working at older ages," says the National Academies.[387]

Legislation to protect older workers from age discrimination, such as the federal Age Discrimination in Employment Act (ADEA) of 1967 in the United States and various state laws that are even more stringent, can also play a role in prolonging the careers of older workers. The ADEA protects people over age forty from discrimination in hiring, firing, promotion, layoff compensation, benefits, job assignments, and training.[388]

Beyond these laws and policies, which are already in place, the National Academies suggest extending affirmative action to include older workers, noting, "There is evidence that affirmative action policies have been successful in boosting employment for other covered groups and, therefore, would likely improve employment prospects for older workers."[389] Governments could also consider implementing policies to subsidize companies that take on or provide accommodations for older workers.

As for policies to promote and support aging in place, there are several possible options. Lawmakers could enact policies to fund and facilitate home modifications, such as the construction of ramps and railings. Or they could craft policies to promote the repurposing of suburban spaces to meet the needs of aging residents, say, converting a vacant strip mall to a medical plaza. Other policies might involve adapting public transit to accommodate older riders, supporting informal caregivers such as friends and family members, and allowing homeowners to draw on their home equity to finance aging in place.

NOTE: There's certainly a place for public policy, but I tend to favor marketplace solutions to these types of problems. I'll talk about these in chapter 10.

CHAPTER 9

IMMIGRATION

Only one policy aimed at deliberately altering a
country's size, population structure, and demographic
rhythms can hope to effect major and beneficial
long-term consequences. This is immigration.

—NICHOLAS EBERSTADT, HENRY WENDT CHAIR IN
POLITICAL ECONOMY, AMERICAN ENTERPRISE INSTITUTE

Increasing fertility and tapping the talent of our older workers are two ways to address the problems associated with aging and declining populations: too few workers, producing too few goods and services, and various cascading effects. But a third tactic could have a more profound effect: increasing immigration.

Immigration, says Nicholas Eberstadt at American Enterprise Institute (AEI), is the *only* policy "aimed at altering a country's size, population structure, and demographic rhythms [that] can hope to effect major and beneficial long-term consequences."[390] The IHME agrees: "For high-income countries with fertility rates lower than the replacement level, the most immediate solution is liberal immigration policies."[391]

These aren't predictions. They're conclusions. The UN estimates that between 2000 and 2020, 80.5 million people migrated to high-income countries. During that same period, births in those countries outnumbered deaths by just 66.2 million.[392] In a similar vein, the US Census Bureau reports that roughly 1 million people migrated to the United States in 2022, while births outnumbered deaths by just 260,000.[393] All this is to say that in these examples, immigration did more to maintain population numbers than fertility did.

Most immigrants are working age or younger. And people who emigrate from low-income countries to high-income ones often have higher fertility rates, at least at first. Eventually—if not in the first generation, then usually in the second—immigrants tend to adopt the fertility habits of their new home, causing their fertility rates to drop. But for a while, liberal immigration policies act as a twofer (or more-fer) of sorts, decreasing a country's median age and OADR.

Jonathan V. Last, author of *What to Expect When No One's Expecting*, observes, "It's sobering to imagine what America's fertility rate would look like today without all of our recent immigrants, both legal and illegal."[394] The same goes for several other developed countries. Yet in recent years, many of these countries, including the United States, have enacted policies to *reduce* immigration.

This chapter discusses why people migrate, the economic benefits of immigration, problems associated with immigration, and the importance of competing to attract new immigrants. It also suggests a way to facilitate the movement of the right immigrants to the right countries based on both their needs.

WHY PEOPLE MIGRATE

Recall from chapter 2 that people generally migrate for one of two reasons. One reason is that political upheaval, war, persecution, environmental degradation, or natural disasters cause conditions at home to degenerate to such a degree that it's simply not safe to stay. This is called *push migration* because circumstances push people out. People who move for these reasons are generally called *refugees* rather than *migrants*.

> **NOTE:** Some people migrate against their will through "force, blackmail, or gross deception," notes Fred Pearce in *The Coming Population Crash*. However, he says these comprise a "significant minority of migrants."[395]

The other main reason people migrate is to capitalize on better opportunities abroad. This occurs when their home country is impoverished, their living conditions are poor, there are too many people, there aren't enough jobs to go around, or they have career aspirations that can only be achieved elsewhere. This type of migration, called *pull migration*, is generally "about strivers looking to cash in on the economic opportunities another country has to offer them and their families," say Darrell Bricker and John Ibbitson in *Empty Planet*.[396] Pearce agrees: "Most migrants are not fleeing poverty so much as seeking wealth. They are aspirational."[397]

> **NOTE:** Immigrants from poorer regions often send money to their relatives back home. In this way, immigration is a win-win, benefiting the immigrant's new country *and* their old one.

INTERNAL MIGRATION

People don't just migrate from one country to another. They also migrate within their own country, usually to capitalize on opportunities outside their community. This is called *internal migration*.

It used to be that most internal migrants moved from rural areas to urban ones. Between 2010 and 2020, more than two-thirds of US counties located outside a metropolitan area experienced population decline.[398] However, because of the high cost of living in major cities and the increased prevalence of remote work as a result of the recent COVID-19 pandemic, this might be changing.

According to the US Census Bureau, between July 2020 and July 2021, major American cities such as New York, Chicago, San Francisco, and Los Angeles shed more than seven hundred thousand residents. Meanwhile, cities such as Phoenix, Houston, Dallas, Austin, and Atlanta attracted more than three hundred thousand new inhabitants. Rural areas and some smaller cities also experienced considerable growth.[399]

This trend, should it continue, could revitalize rural areas, towns, and smaller cities. But it might have downsides too, most notably aging populations and labor shortages in major cities.

ECONOMIC BENEFITS OF IMMIGRATION

Many people view immigration in strictly humanitarian terms—a way to support refugees fleeing from conflict, looking for political cover, or being displaced by a natural disaster. There's also "a strong moral case to allow families from low-income countries to move to a richer country, where they can improve their lot by an order of magnitude," says Derek Thompson of the *Atlantic*.[400]

But accepting immigrants isn't just about humanitarianism and morality. There's a powerful economic case for immigration. Immigration can help stave off the economic problems associated with aging and declining populations—with immediate effect. When it comes to immigrants, "You need them as much as they need you," say Bricker and Ibbitson."[401]

> **NOTE:** Immigration is not merely a matter of humanity and justice but also of economics and future prosperity.

In the United States, immigrants often take on "low-skill" roles: domestic worker, kitchen staff, construction laborer, farmhand, garbage collector, landscaper, caregiver, and so on. Because these are the types of immigrant workers that many Americans encounter most frequently, they tend to assume that most immigrants fit this profile. Americans might even look down on these immigrants, even though they perform important jobs that are roundly rejected by native-born people.

In reality these types of workers comprise less than half of all legal immigrants to the United States. A greater percentage are considered "high-skilled." They fill significant gaps in demand for professionals such as healthcare providers, tech workers, and so on. Many of these high-skilled immigrants arrive in the United States "during their peak productive years after another society has usually borne the cost of raising them," says Shikha Dalmia at the *New York Times*. In this way, they bestow a "one-time fiscal windfall on America."[402]

> **NOTE:** The vast majority (79 percent) of immigrants who have arrived in the United States since 2010 are of working age and have an OADR of just 5.8.[403] That's a lot lower than the OADR of the US population at large, which in 2020 was a whopping 24.9![404] In general, more immigrants means a more favorable OADR.

Beyond accepting important jobs that might otherwise go undone, some immigrants start successful and impactful businesses of their own. A 2018 study by the National Foundation for American Policy revealed that immigrants launched 55 percent (50 of 91) of all privately owned start-up companies in the United States valued at $1 billion or more; the collective value of these 50 companies was $248 billion; and each of these companies generated more than 1,200 jobs on average.[405] Immigrants or the children of immigrants also founded nearly half (219) of all companies listed in the 2022 Fortune 500.

The bottom line: At least right now, says economist Paul Krugman, "It's an exaggeration, but one with some truth, to say that immigrants are saving the U.S. economy" and that "immigration is, from an economic point of view, a good thing all around."[406]

PROBLEMS WITH IMMIGRATION

Some experts see immigration as the easiest and most effective way to address shortfalls in the population as a whole and in the labor force in particular, especially in the short term. And yet many countries, even ones facing imminent dramatic demographic decline, "have not adopted immigration as a compensating strategy," says the IHME.[407] In fact, several of these countries, including the United States, have recently enacted policies to *limit* immigration.

> **NOTE:** Economists estimate that because of anti-immigration policies enacted during President Donald Trump's term in office, the United States took in two million fewer immigrants than it would have otherwise, sending employers scrambling to fill empty jobs.[408]

NATIONALISM AND POPULISM

A common reason countries reject immigrants is that their "desire to maintain a linguistic and culturally homogenous society has outweighed the economic, fiscal, and geopolitical risks of declining populations," says the IHME.[409] This is a polite way of describing xenophobia (a dislike or prejudice against people from other countries), nationalism (whereby people identify with their own nation or group and its interests to the exclusion or detriment of others), and populism (often linked to "nationalist nostalgia" or to "frustration over declines in status or welfare," says the *Economist*).[410]

Xenophobia, nationalism, and populism have spiked in recent years, particularly on the far-right end of the political spectrum. Why?

Well, there are lots of reasons, but one of them relates to low fertility and population decline. "As rich countries have fewer babies," says Thompson, "they need immigration to grow their prime-age workforces. But as the foreign-born share of the population rises, xenophobia often festers." He continues, "Far-right parties thrive by politicizing the perceived threat of the foreign-born to national culture."[411]

This scenario has played out time and time again, not just in the distant past but lately too. This is particularly true in Europe. I already discussed Hungarian prime minister Viktor Orbán's recent warnings against race mixing; Orbán also, in his own words, "stands for an openly anti-immigration policy."[412] Far-right Finnish politicians have gained ground by stoking fears of immigrants (many of whom are refugees).[413] In France, concerns about immigration and the country's growing Muslim population fueled the ascendance of ultraright-wing politician Marine Le Pen, who was very nearly elected president in 2022. Prime Minister Giorgia Meloni of Italy, who has warned Italians against the dangers of "ethnic replacement,"[414] was more successful. A surge of Arabic and African refugees drove voters to grant her party—described by political scientists as anti-immigrant, nationalist, nativist, authoritarian, and even neofascist—control over parliament. And many blame Brexit on British nativist fears.

Of course, this scenario also played out in the United States, where Donald Trump became president in 2016 after launching his campaign with a speech denigrating Mexican immigrants. Trump's anti-immigrant message resonated especially well in areas that had experienced significant demographic change over a short period of time. For example, according to 2016 analysis by the *Wall Street Journal*, counties in Iowa, Indiana, Wisconsin, Illinois, and Minnesota that had attracted large numbers of Latino newcomers over a short period overwhelmingly favored Trump in the 2016 presidential election.[415]

It's no coincidence that many of these counties were situated in more rural areas. Anti-immigrant views plague places where "populations are sparse or shrinking" and "economies are stagnant," say Philip Auerswald and Joon Yun at the *New York Times*,[416] even if immigrants don't actually displace any of the people who are already there.[417]

> **NOTE:** Western countries aren't the only ones that reject immigrants. Eastern countries such as Japan, Korea, China, and Taiwan do too. "The people of these countries see themselves as racially homogeneous, and see that homogeneity as something to prize and protect," say Bricker and Ibbitson.[418]

SCHRÖDINGER'S IMMIGRANT

Some Americans believe that immigrants steal jobs. Oddly, many of those same Americans also believe that immigrants hog government resources. The Urban Dictionary calls this paradox *Schrödinger's Immigrant*: "The elusive non-white non-US citizen who is capable of both taking all of the jobs from hard-working Americans who are left unemployed, while also at the same time sitting around doing nothing and collecting welfare and other government benefits, thereby leeching off the American taxpayers."[419]

In reality, the opposite is true. Many immigrants work low-wage jobs that few (if any) native-born people want. They're not stealing those jobs; they're the only ones willing to do them.

> Moreover, as mentioned, many immigrants "are powerful job creators," says Professor Ben Jones at the Kellogg School of Management. In fact, immigrants "create more jobs than they take." The result: "Immigrants actually improve the economic outcomes for native-born workers," says Jones.[420]

ASSIMILATION

Immigrants might speak different languages, follow different social and cultural norms, practice different religions, and perhaps even possess different physical features from the existing inhabitants in their new country. This might not be a problem in major cities with heterogeneous populations. But in smaller cities and rural areas, where populations tend to be more homogeneous, many locals see these differences as a failure to assimilate. This "failure" in turn amplifies any populist views those locals might already hold.

Assimilation is difficult. For most of us, our identities are influenced, even defined, by our place of origin. Shedding that identity is like shedding a vital part of ourselves.

Assimilation also takes time. A first-generation immigrant might never fully assimilate. They will likely continue to speak their own language (or speak their new language with an accent), follow their own social and cultural norms, and practice their own religion, at least to some degree. Their children, however, will almost certainly adopt the language, norms, and possibly even the religious practices of the new country and their grandchildren even more.

In recent years, at least in the United States, views on assimilation have begun to shift. Now instead of seeing the United States as a melting pot, some Americans think of it as more like a salad bowl. Within this salad bowl, says Bruce Thornton at Stanford's Hoover Institution, various ethnic groups "coexist in their separate identities like the ingredients in a salad, bound together only by the 'dressing' of law and the market."[421]

The salad bowl metaphor reflects a growing emphasis on *multiculturalism*, which calls for the preservation of different cultural identities within a broader, unified society. "To combat depopulation, nations must embrace both immigration *and* multiculturalism," say Bricker and Ibbitson. They describe immigration without multiculturalism as "a recipe for exclusion, ghettoization, marginalization, violence, and ultimately, the worst of fates: the collapse of the public square, the inability of different groups within a society to share space and assumptions and values together."[422]

SHORT-TERM SOLUTION

Liberal immigration laws can help address population decline—but perhaps only in the short term. Because of recent developments in emerging economies, immigrants may soon be very difficult to attract. "Whether you view immigration as a blessing or a curse," says Last, "you should understand that it may be temporary."[423]

One development is that the regions that typically supply immigrants (India, Latin America, and Africa) now experience lower fertility rates themselves. The UNPD reports that India's fertility rate plunged from 5.73 in 1950 to 2.05 in 2020.[424] That's below the replacement rate. Fertility rates in Latin America and the Caribbean fell even more during that same period, from 5.80 to 1.90.[425] Again, below the replacement rate. And in Africa, fertility rates dropped from a high of 6.72 in 1968 to 4.36 in 2022. That's above the replacement rate, but it's falling faster than expected.[426] Eventually—and this is crucial—these regions will experience the same problems as advanced economies: aging societies and perhaps even population decline. "At that point," says Last, "These countries will have their own labor shortages, meaning emigration from the region may significantly diminish."[427]

Another development is that in many of these areas, thanks in large part to globalization but also to lower birth rates, poverty is declining, and the standard of living is improving. If this trend continues, and it almost certainly will, fewer people will feel compelled to search out better opportunities elsewhere.

In some places this shift has already begun. For example, in recent years the number of Mexicans migrating to the United States has dropped, primarily because the 1994 passage of the North American Free Trade Agreement dramatically improved Mexico's economic outlook. Indeed, between 2009 and 2019, more Mexicans *left* the United States than arrived.[428] (This trend has recently reversed, however, as Mexico's economy has deteriorated, and violence there has increased.)

WHERE DO IMMIGRANTS COME FROM?

Most immigrants move from countries with emerging economies and a high fertility rate to countries with advanced economies and a low fertility rate. As a country blossoms from the former to the latter, the number of people who emigrate from it tends to decline.

Countries in Latin America, MENA, sub-Saharan Africa, and the Indian subcontinent currently export the most immigrants. Soon, though, dropping fertility rates will likely knock most

Latin American countries off this list, leaving India, MENA, and sub-Saharan Africa to produce the bulk of our next generation of immigrants.

Even these regions won't be able to supply immigrants forever, though, and they might run out of surplus population sooner than people think. As mentioned, India's fertility rate has already fallen below replacement levels. And there's reason to think Africa's population could nose-dive within a generation too because of increasing urbanization and higher education rates among girls and women.

COMPETING FOR IMMIGRANTS

Even as some countries reject immigrants, others compete to attract them. Leading the charge is Canada. Its immigration policy "is expressly meant to offset its aging population and low birthrates," says Dalmia at the *New York Times.*"[429]

In 2022 Canada, whose current population is roughly 39 million people, admitted a record-breaking number of immigrants: 431,645. But that record won't last long. The country has set ambitious goals to welcome even more in 2023 (465,000), 2024 (485,000), and 2025 (500,000).[430]

In this effort Canada will almost certainly succeed. "Canada goes to comparatively great lengths to help immigrants assimilate by providing them with orientation programs, skills training, social services, and pathways to citizenship," says Amelia Cheatham at the Council on Foreign Relations. Thanks to this level of support, says

Cheatham, Canada has become "one of the most sought-after destinations for immigrants, with high rates of immigrant satisfaction and naturalization."[431]

Even Quebec, a historic stronghold for anti-immigrant views due to its strong sense of cultural identity, has begun welcoming immigrants. A recent *New York Times* article by Norimitsu Onishi profiled a rural Quebecois town that passed an anti-immigrant code of conduct in 2007, only to reverse it a decade later because of low birth rates, an aging population, and acute labor shortages. "We now want as many immigrants as possible," the town's mayor told Onishi.[432]

> **NOTE:** Cities and towns regularly compete to attract new residents. Auerswald and Yun describe one Italian village that is so "desperate to reverse two decades of population decline" that "if you accept [the mayor's] invitation to move there, he will pay you about $2,300."[433]

Countries that want to weather the coming demographic storm should mimic Canada's methods. So far, though, only a few have: Portugal created a new type of visa to attract immigrants to fill construction and tourism jobs, Australia simplified its immigration system and increased its quotas, and Spain relaxed several immigration rules.

What about the United States? The United States absorbed more than a million legal immigrants in 2022, but its total population is 334 million, nearly ten times that of Canada. The United States could, and should, take in far more. Apart from helping to solve the various problems associated with aging and declining populations that we've discussed throughout this book, replenishing our graying workforce with immigrants would provide us with a critical competitive edge from a geopolitical and economic standpoint. This is especially true with respect to China. Many economists claim that China's economy could soon eclipse our own. But if we manage to maintain stable population numbers through immigration, then China will find itself at a distinct disadvantage when its own population plummets in the years to come.

A few US states are beginning to recognize the need to attract immigrants, including some states you might not expect, such as Iowa. Because of shortages in "key mid-skill industries like health care, information and technology and tourism and hospitality," say Kristie De Peña, Robert Leonard, and David Oman in the *New York Times*, employers in Iowa "are begging for workers."[434] In response, Iowa governor Kim Reynolds, a Republican, has introduced a program to attract refugees from around the world.

LEGAL VERSUS ILLEGAL IMMIGRATION

It's important to distinguish between *legal immigration*, whereby documented immigrants enter a new country through the proper channels, and *illegal immigration*, in which undocumented immigrants slip in undetected.

Illegal immigration often brings with it a host of problems. For example, "Illegal immigration creates downward pressure at the low end of the wage scale," notes Last. It also "puts stress on social services for those most in need and makes it hard for natives who aren't college graduates to earn a living."[435] (That being said, many undocumented immigrants also pay into social security—money they'll never get back.)

Few politicians are in favor of illegal immigration, but most have historically supported the presence of *legal*, or documented, immigrants. Recently, however, that's changed, at least in the United States. Some American politicians, particularly on the far right, now seek to limit *all* immigration.

Many advanced economies, including the United States and Europe, rely heavily on immigrant labor, legal or not. So when a country limits legal immigration, illegal immigration tends to spike. "The current practice of barring most legal migrants while letting millions of others slip illegally through the back door serves only the worst interest and promotes lawlessness," says Gregory A. Maniatis of Open Society Foundations. Therefore, "Smugglers are enriched, immigrants work in oppressive conditions, and xenophobia runs rampant."[436] That needs fixing.

GLOBAL HR DEPARTMENT: MATCHING IMMIGRANTS WITH JOBS

Some parts of the world have too few people, and other parts have too many. "Importing and exporting people is an obvious safety valve for both," says Pearce.[437] However, simply moving warm bodies from one place to another won't do. Instead, we need some way to bring the right people, with the right skills, to the right place. Otherwise, everything falls apart.

That's what's happening in Germany: everything's falling apart. Germany's population is aging fast. As older workers retire over the next decade or so, they will leave an estimated seven million jobs vacant. So Germany needs people. But Germany *has* people. Since 2015 Germany has welcomed millions of immigrants, many of them war refugees from Syria and Ukraine. Problem solved, right? Wrong. Unfortunately, "Many refugees are poorly suited for jobs in Germany's highly skilled labor market," says Tom Fairless at the *Wall Street Journal.* As a result, "Half of German businesses say they are cutting back their operations or relocating abroad because they can't find enough workers."[438]

Germany isn't alone. This is a big problem in lots of advanced economies. But I believe it's one that could be solved through the development of what I think of as a global HR department. Although difficult to frame and execute, such a resource could create pipelines of workers with specific skills for export to countries that need them. "Immigration solves labor shortages in the developed world, and emigration solves job shortages in the developing world," says Kai McNamee at NPR. "It's a win-win."[439]

I'm not the first guy to think this way. Lots of NGOs work on matching the right people with the right places on a global scale. But as important as these types of organizations are, I wonder if a marketplace solution might work better. Businesses are notoriously more agile than NGOs and often more innovative too. And of course, any business that could develop a global HR tool would be *enormously* profitable. Economist Lant Pritchett envisions an industry that "recruits, prepares, places, protects" migrant workers."[440] I think he's onto something.

NOTE: Amazon developed AWS to address its own internal server workload needs and, in doing so, spawned an entire billion-dollar industry. Perhaps some company might stumble onto a global HR solution in a similar fashion.

Of course, building a global HR exchange might be impossible. After all, many countries remain staunchly anti-immigrant, and that's unlikely to change anytime soon. But eventually, all countries will need to "start rethinking their policies on migration, workforces and economic development to address the challenges presented by demographic change," says Dr. Christopher Murray of the IHME.[441] The sooner we do this, the better off we'll be.

CHAPTER 10

THE ROLE OF BUSINESS

The deep reform that I believe business must lead ... is not just about persistently thinking and acting with a next-generation view—although that's a key part of it. It's about rewiring the fundamental ways we govern, manage, and lead corporations. It's also about changing how we view business's value and its role in society.

—DOMINIC BARTON, *HARVARD BUSINESS REVIEW*

n 1969 more than half of the global population lived in extreme poverty.[442] "At best, they had barely enough money to eat and pay for necessities like clothes," says the *Economist*. "At worst, they starved."[443]

In the half century since, the free-market system has "fueled unprecedented economic growth around the world ... lifted hundreds of millions of people out of poverty and cut the global poverty rate by two-thirds," say Anthony B. Kim and Patrick Tyrrell of the Heritage

Foundation.[444] Indeed, says President Barack Obama—who, by the way, operates on the polar opposite end of the political spectrum from Kim and Tyrrell—"Free markets have created more wealth than any system in history. They have lifted billions out of poverty."[445]

In the same way free-market capitalism has eased extreme poverty, I believe it can facilitate a less painful transition to our new demographic reality: aging and declining populations.

"Capitalism is not just about accumulation," says conservative commentator Arthur Brooks. "At its best, it's about aspiration."[446] Capitalism calls on us to take big swings to solve big problems and in doing so create a better world. Well, aging and declining populations definitely present some big problems: too few people, producing too few goods and services, and various cascading effects. These are problems that capitalism—that business—must aspire to solve.

In practical terms, solving these problems entails retaining and maximizing whatever workforce remains. Companies will have to pay employees a living wage, provide safe work environments, and in countries that lack universal healthcare, offer access to affordable insurance. These practices are so obvious I won't even bother discussing them further.

Beyond that, businesses must support working parents, accommodate older employees, and expand their pool of "acceptable" workers. They'll also need to invest in technological innovation to offset the shrinking labor pool. And they'll have to reject corporate short-termism in favor of a longer view. That's what this chapter is about.

NOTE: Attracting immigrants is also important, but I believe government has more levers to achieve this than business.

SUPPORTING WORKING PARENTS

In advanced economies, both men and women work. These economies can't function otherwise. But many workers, men and women alike, struggle to reconcile job and family duties. According to a 2019 Pew Research survey, roughly half of parents in the United States say that "being a working parent makes it harder for them to be a good parent." At the same time, roughly the same percentage of parents report that "at times they feel they can't give 100% at work."[447]

The issue is this: The goal of any business is to grow. And rightfully so! That's how businesses survive. But "When growth becomes a supreme good," says Yuval Noah Harari in *Sapiens*, "unrestricted by any other ethical considerations, it can easily lead to catastrophe."[448]

Is the struggle to reconcile job and family duties a catastrophe? No. But it does cause lots of couples with careers to have fewer children than they'd like (or none at all). And it forces many parents who *do* have kids to drop out of the workforce to care for them—even if they don't want to.

Parents who remain employed don't just struggle with work-life balance. Many also face discrimination at work. "Employers may discriminate based on family responsibilities when they deny employment or promotions, harass, pay less, or otherwise take negative employment action against an employee because of the employee's family responsibilities," says Workplace Fairness, a nonprofit organization that promotes workers' rights.[449]

Mothers are particularly vulnerable to workplace discrimination. Some companies even discriminate against women who *might someday become* moms. Like a manager at one company said to rationalize his aversion to hiring young women: "First comes love, then comes marriage, then comes flextime and a baby carriage."[450] (Surprise! This company was sued.)

> **NOTE:** "Capitalism is good for people, but not so great for the family," says Jonathan V. Last in *What to Expect When No One's Expecting.*[451]

To stave off labor shortages that will inevitably arise because of aging and declining populations—and maybe even boost fertility rates (which would boost population numbers down the line)—companies must accommodate the needs of working parents. At a bare minimum, this means offering paid parental leave for moms *and* dads upon the birth or adoption of a child. Then when parents return to work, "Working hours might be negotiated between the employer and the employee with a view to the employee's family responsibilities," says demographer Peter McDonald.[452] And of course, companies should allow for short-term absences—for example, to care for a sick child or attend a school event.

Remote work arrangements can also help employees reconcile job and family duties. For one thing, when employees work remotely, they recoup time they normally lose commuting, which they can then spend with their loved ones. For another, working from home makes it easier to perform household and family duties. Remote work arrangements could even free up workers to live nearer to family members, such as parents or grandparents, who might be in a position to provide various types of support such as childcare or running errands.

> **NOTE:** "Telecommuting wouldn't just make it easier for people to have families," says Last. "It could return intergenerational family relationships to their traditional form."[453]

It's particularly important for companies to ensure that their corporate culture does not punish parents for fulfilling familial obligations. It's no good offering generous parental leave, flexible scheduling, and free time for school events if parents are made to feel guilty for using these benefits. On a related note, companies should also avoid scheduling meetings very early or very late in the day to accommodate parents who need to drop off or pick up their kids from school and should keep team building and social events within regular working hours.

> **It's particularly important for companies to ensure that their corporate culture does not punish parents for fulfilling familial obligations.**

These practices don't just benefit employees who are (or want to be) parents. They benefit companies too. For example, according to Gallup, companies that allow employees to work from home at least part of the time experience higher employee engagement. This is a big deal. "When employees are engaged," says Gallup, "their performance soars."[454] Similarly, flexible work arrangements designed to assist families improve employee retention, not just among parents but everyone else too.[455]

> **NOTE:** Retaining existing staff and ensuring they remain engaged will become increasingly critical as our labor force contracts.

ACCOMMODATING OLDER WORKERS

Supporting working parents is one way to combat a contracting workforce. Another is accommodating older workers so they are willing, able, and eager to remain employed for longer. "In an aging society with slowing population growth," says Nicholas Eberstadt at the AEI, "making the most out of existing manpower, including older workers, is of the essence."[456]

"Employees can signal the value they place on retaining older workers through the policies and practices they enact within the workplace," says the National Academies.[457] They recommend the following various practices to encourage older workers to stick around:

- **ACCOMMODATION PRACTICES:** These offset possible declines in the physical and cognitive capabilities of older workers. They involve improving ergonomics (for example, providing larger computer screens to assist aging eyes), adapting jobs to minimize physical strain, and allowing for flexible work arrangements such as remote work.

- **DEVELOPMENTAL PRACTICES:** These provide older workers with opportunities to learn, develop, and advance. They might include training in new technologies or more efficient work processes.

- **RETENTION AND EXIT PRACTICES:** These permit older workers to retire gradually and in phases—working fewer and fewer hours or handling a smaller and smaller workload over time—instead of all at once. They might also allow for contingent work arrangements, in which older workers stay on as independent contractors, allowing them greater flexibility and autonomy.

> **NOTE:** Workplace flexibility—when, where, and how much to work—is "important to workers of all ages, including older workers," says the National Academies.[458]

- **AGE-INCLUSIVE PRACTICES:** These ensure all employees, regardless of age, feel welcome and accepted. They involve actively combating ageist stereotypes about older workers— for example, that older workers lack stamina, are unmotivated, underperform, oppose change, and resist training—and recognizing the value of more seasoned employees.

Older workers are assets, not liabilities. They are our "most qualified, most experienced individuals," says Fred Pearce in *The Coming Population Crash*. "Companies with a decent portion of older workers are more productive than those addicted to youth," explains Pearce, because "age brings experience and wisdom that complements the attributes of the young."[459]

Granted, when it comes to purely physical work or work that is dull or repetitive, performance might decline with age. But "More challenging jobs that profit from experience, teamwork, and insights into human nature—as well as sustained interest—may increase performance with age (or experience)," says the National Academies.[460]

Keeping older workers on the job could help solve many problems associated with aging and declining populations. But it might create some problems too, such as hampering the ability of younger workers to advance. According to a 2022 survey by the Nationwide Retirement Institute, more than one-third of private sector employers in the United States say delayed retirements affect their ability to hire and promote young talent.[461] This aligns with the findings of an earlier study at the Kellogg School of Business, which indicated that in firms with older workers who postponed retirement, younger workers received fewer promotions, and their wages grew more slowly.[462]

The most effective way for companies to clear this hurdle is to grow faster—for example, by expanding into new markets—to create more high-level jobs for younger employees. If that's not possible, firms will likely need to mollify junior staff with higher salaries, stock options, or bonuses.

NOTE: It would behoove governments to incentivize businesses to hire older workers—for example, by offering subsidies.

THE IMPORTANCE OF MEANINGFUL WORK

According to a 2015 survey, nearly one-fourth of all US workers, including many older workers, reported that it was "very important" that their work be "morally, personally, or spiritually significant."[463] They wanted a "quality job"—in other words, meaningful work.

Sadly, these jobs are hard to come by, even in advanced economies. Indeed, says author David Graeber in his book *Bullshit Jobs: A Theory*, many jobs are "so completely pointless, unnecessary, or pernicious that even the employee cannot justify [their] existence."

Maybe that's a bit harsh. Then again, maybe not. Half of all respondents to a 2013 poll by the *Harvard Business Review* described their work as having "no meaning and significance."[464] And a 2015 survey by YouGov revealed that more than one-third of working adults in Great Britain said their jobs did not "make a meaningful contribution to the world."[465] On a related note, as recently as 2019, 50 percent of US workers described their job as "bad."[466]

It's not all lousy news. Innovative technologies such as automation and AI could soon take over jobs that involve maximum drudgery. (More on that in a moment.) But businesses will still need to do a better job of highlighting how each employee's daily tasks connect to the company's mission and of ensuring that said mission is meaningful.

TURNING TO TECHNOLOGY

As our workforce contracts, companies that support working parents and accommodate older workers will have an advantage over companies that don't. Eventually, though, as populations in more and more countries begin to age and decline, all companies will need to operate with fewer people—*without* falling behind in terms of economic growth.

Maintaining current growth rates, let alone increasing them, will require "a significant increase in the rates of growth of productivity per worker," say Charles Goodhart and Manoj Pradhan in *The Great Demographic Reversal*.[467] Achieving this will entail the adoption of technologies such as automation, robotics, the cloud, big data, AI, the Internet of Things, and more.

> **NOTE:** These are just technologies we've invented so far. Necessity being the mother of invention, I predict that additional innovative technologies—things we haven't even thought of yet—will emerge in the coming years.

Unless you've spent the last forty years living under a rock on a desert island, you're no doubt aware that countless companies have already adopted these and other technologies to improve efficiency and push up profits. You also likely realize that as a result, the need for certain types of workers has been reduced or even eliminated—think assembly-line workers, cashiers, bank tellers, pharmacy technicians, and more. But what you might not realize is that by the mid-2030s, 30 percent of *all* jobs could potentially be automated.[468]

If one of those jobs is yours, that sounds bad. So bad, in fact, that you might agree with the 48 percent of adults in the United States who believe automation has "mostly hurt American workers" and the nearly 60 percent who say that "there should be limits on the number of jobs that businesses can replace with machines."[469]

But the reality is, as our workforce contracts, "We will need all the automation we can get," say Goodhart and Pradhan. Indeed, "The disruption from technology that so many fear so much in the advanced economies is actually an imperative without which the damage to global growth could well be far worse."[470] This is why countries such as South Korea, Japan, and Germany, all with very low fertility rates and very high median ages, are "at the forefront of developing robots and artificial intelligence for the workplace," says John Yoon at the *New York Times*.[471] (In case you're wondering, these same countries also boast some of the lowest unemployment numbers on earth.[472])

> **NOTE:** Technologies such as automation, robotics, and AI are important solutions to problems associated with aging societies.

Technology won't replace humans. "Automation is a global complement for labour, not a substitute," say Goodhart and Pradhan.[473] Still, just as the invention of the automobile eventually rendered carriage makers obsolete, the proliferation of novel technologies will require many of us to develop new skills or even change careers completely.

The question is, what types of new skills should we develop? According to Andrew McAfee of the MIT Initiative on the Digital Economy, the answer is, "good old-fashioned human skills," such as negotiating, motivating, persuading, and coordinating.[474] Beyond that, says Rich Lesser of the Boston Consulting Group, workers should alter their mindset from "learning something" to "learning how to learn."[475]

Admittedly, adapting to technological changes won't be easy. But there are upsides. Here's one: just as early automakers sparked the formation of entire industries to supply them, whole new trades will materialize to support emerging technologies. So there will be plenty of brand-new opportunities available for anyone willing to shift gears and change lanes.

Also, technology facilitates remote work. This helps workers, of course, by enabling them to live where they like. But it also helps businesses because it expands the pool of possible employees. If an employee who lives thirty miles from company headquarters can operate effectively, so can an employee who lives three hundred or even three thousand miles away.

Finally, says Ulrich Spiesshofer, CEO of ABB Group, "If you use technology right, it elevates the nature of work."[476] With technology, we can shift staff from work that is tedious, boring, and repetitive into more interesting, engaging, and meaningful roles—that is to say quality (read: not bad) jobs.

REJECTING CORPORATE SHORT-TERMISM

The problem of aging and declining populations is a long-term one. But most businesses today suffer from short-termism. That is, they place "an excessive focus on short-term results at the expense of long-term interests,"[477] says the CFA Institute, which promotes ethical, educational, and professional standards in the global investment services industry.

> **NOTE:** Short-termism emerged in the 1980s, when traders began investing in companies based primarily on their quarterly performance, which in turn forced corporate managers to concentrate almost solely on quarterly earnings.[478]

According to Penn State professor J. Randall Woodridge, short-termism manifests in various ways. For example, managers might become risk averse, or forsake longer-term investments such as in research and development, to keep short-term earnings strong. Or they might turn to financial instruments such as stock buybacks (which, by the way, were illegal until 1982) or play other "financial games" to boost short-term financial performance.

> **NOTE:** Many politicians also suffer from short-termism due to electoral cycles. This doesn't help matters.

The results of short-termism are pernicious. Product development decisions might show "little imagination," says Woodridge. Worse, "innovation is discouraged" in favor of "imitation and backward integration because of their more predictable results."[479] The late business guru Peter Drucker described these types of decisions as "costly, if not suicidal."[480]

To combat the effects of aging and declining populations, including a shrinking labor pool and potentially shrinking markets, companies *must* reject short-termism. This means making long-term plans for staffing and long-term investments in innovation to improve efficiency.

> **NOTE:** Just as agricultural innovations averted widespread famine during the green revolution of the 1960s and 1970s, innovations today can help us offset problems associated with aging and declining populations. Simply put, we *must* devote resources to ideas, short-termism be damned.

Taking a long view brings benefits beyond simply adapting to aging and declining populations. A 2017 study by McKinsey Global Institute and FCLTGlobal revealed that between 2001 and 2014, companies with a long-term mindset "consistently outperformed their industry peers across almost every financial measure that matters," say Dominic Barton, James Manyika, and Sarah Keohane Williamson in the *Harvard Business Review*.[481] Moreover, their revenue was 47 percent higher, their earnings growth was 36 percent higher, their profit growth was 81 percent higher, and total shareholder returns were higher too.[482] If the entire economy had performed at this same level, say Barton et al., "U.S. GDP over the past decade might well have grown by an additional $1 trillion."[483]

> **NOTE:** Long-termism also promotes trust among customers *and* employees, something that will become increasingly important as the effects of aging and declining populations become manifest.

This won't be easy. Short-termism has become positively entrenched. But companies that fail to make this shift will find themselves forced to adopt a new way of thinking: no-termism, because they'll be out of business.

CONCLUSION

F or generations, demographic doomers have warned the general public that our human population is spiraling out of control. And despite considerable data to the contrary, organizations such as the UN that monitor global population trends have failed to rewrite this narrative. If anything, they've doubled down on it. According to the UN's most recent projections, the human population—currently 8 billion people—will peak at more than 10.4 billion in 2086.[484] That's their story, and they're sticking to it.

To me, that story is a tall tale. My own analysis shows that our global population will peak much sooner and at a much lower number. And I predict that the populations of most developed countries will age and decline much earlier than expected.

These findings are significant. If the UN's projections are wrong, then every entity that relies on those projections to make consequential decisions—say, a municipal government deciding how many schools or hospitals to build, or a company considering where to invest key resources—will be basing those decisions on flawed facts. Meanwhile, because these same entities believe they have more time to plan for problems associated with aging and declining populations, they'll find themselves wholly unprepared when those problems arise (if they haven't already) in a matter of years rather than decades.

These problems, the ones I've talked about throughout this book, well, they're big. And when faced with big problems, no matter what they are, it's easy to become pessimistic. That's why so many people look to the future with such a profound sense of gloom. They believe our problems are unsolvable, that all our good days are behind us, that things can only get worse.

There's no reason to believe we can't solve—or better yet, avert—problems associated with aging societies and population decline too.

Adopting this stance will not help us avert the problems associated with aging and declining populations. And anyway, it just isn't true. Humans are "intelligent beings who are uniquely capable of innovating their way out of pressing problems,"[485] say Marian Tupy and Gale Pooley in *Superabundance*.

We've solved countless big problems, for the whole of our history. We suffered from cold, so we mastered fire. Unable to fully exploit our environment using just our bare hands, we developed tools. After one too many meaty mammoths eluded our grasp, we designed weapons. Farming, villages, trade, science, medicine—our ancestors invented each of these to tackle some big problem. There's no reason to believe we can't solve—or better yet, avert—problems associated with aging societies and population decline too.

> **NOTE:** We mustn't panic about what's to come. "Panic can lead to hasty policy and human tragedy," writes Wang Feng of the *New York Times*.[486] But we must prepare.

Ultimately, averting the problems associated with aging and declining populations—while still enjoying the various benefits these changes might bring, such as lower carbon emissions, more plentiful resources, improved income and wealth equality, better jobs for native-born workers, more mobility for migrants, and so on—will be a bit like landing a plane. Sure, every pilot hopes for a long, smooth runway on a clear, calm day. But I suspect what we're facing is something more like the controlled crash that a flyer experiences when they drop a C-130 Hercules onto the flight deck of an aircraft carrier in rough seas: a bracing jolt and zero room for error. That's our best-case scenario if we prepare, we problem-solve, and everything goes *right*.

So how do we do that? How do we make sure everything goes right, especially here in the United States, in our current era of extreme political polarization? Well, I won't sugarcoat it: it'll be hard. "Decades of accumulating social and political dysfunction have left America less favorably poised for, and perhaps also less capable of seizing, the advantages of the new demographic era ahead of us than we were a generation ago," says Eberstadt.[487]

The fact is, we don't have a choice. If we want our kids to flourish, if we want to sustain our economy and maintain our way of life, if we believe, as I do, that it's our responsibility to make the world a better place, then we must confront the effects of aging and declining populations, not tomorrow, not next year, not after the next election cycle but now. The sooner we start, the less painful these changes will be. And just like the pilot of that C-130 Hercules needs the cooperation of everyone on that aircraft carrier to land that plane, we'll need all hands on deck to forestall this global crisis, not just demographers and government leaders but everyday citizens like you and me. Together, we can get it done. So let's get started.

ACKNOWLEDGMENTS

I find it difficult to get outside of my "comfort zone." It requires a level of intention and vulnerability that often seems insurmountable. Fear of failure and embarrassment is often the biggest obstacle that needs to be overcome.

I have never written a book before. This is completely foreign territory for me, and I'm not exactly sure how the story is going to turn out. Aristotle teaches us that intentionality is an essential component of realizing potential.

I have found intentional vulnerability to be a powerful thing, and I have tried to embrace it whenever I can. I feel encouraged to try something new because as Aristotle also notes, realizing human potential involves nurturing and support. True potential cannot be realized without it.

This project would never have been possible if it weren't for the incredible dedication of my family and friends.

I'd like to express my most sincere appreciation to my wife, Julia. She has been my strongest and most avid supporter. Her tireless efforts and encouragement have given me strength and confidence. Thank you, Juls, for allowing me to do what I do and being by my side while doing it.

This book is about the future, and the future involves my children. I feel a sense of duty when considering the world we pass on to the next generation. Thank you, Mom and Dad, for instilling in me a desire to excel and the work ethic to get it done. Parenting comes with such responsibility, yet it is very empowering as well.

Thank you to my children—Ella, Jack, and Julia—as they have inspired me to do my part in making the world a better place.

So many of my friends have consistently showed genuine interest and have kept me engaged through provocative discussions. Many of the conversations started with "You're studying what? Why?"

The periodic check-ins from Kevin Carroll and Marc Miller and their slight nudgings of encouragement were very helpful.

Two of my champions, Doug Moon and Andy Coughlin, have been relentless supporters. Their initial skepticism turned to unwavering conviction and has been incredibly important to my continued focus.

Help comes in many ways. Expressions of interest and a willingness to help along like Kris Meyer has done for me. Or the technical help in building models like Greg Sheldon has done. Or the help in assembling it together in a communicable package like Spencer Collier has done. I appreciate all of it.

I was always stronger in math and science growing up. English not so much, and writing has never come easy to me. I met my writing partner, Kate Shoup, when starting this project. I feel privileged to have worked with her on this book. She's smart and insightful and has really helped me refine my thoughts into words. Thank you, Kate, for giving me a voice.

None of this happens without the spark and initial curiosity. And for that, I have Rick Varieur to thank. He has given me the gift of understanding. An absolute friend and a person I admire immensely. You believe in me. You love me. And I feel blessed.

ENDNOTES

---

1   "World Population to Reach 8 Billion on 15 November 2022," United Nations Department of Economic and Social Affairs, n.d., https://www.un.org/en/desa/world-population-reach-8-billion-15-november-2022.

2   Alena Botros, "The World's Baby Shortfall Is So Bad That the Labor Shortage Will Last for Years, Major Employment Firms Predict," November 17 2022, https://fortune.com/2022/11/17/declining-birth-rate-labor-shortage-workforce-population-glassdoor-indeed-report/.

Chapter 1

3   Thomas Hobbes, *Leviathan or the Matter, Forme and Power of a Commonwealth Ecclesiastical and Civil* (London, 1651).

4   John Kotre and Elizabeth Hall, *Seasons of Life: Our Dramatic Journey from Birth to Death* (Ann Arbor: University of Michigan Press, 1997).

5   Francis E. Johnston and Charles E. Snow, "The Reassessment of the Age and Sex of the Indian Knoll Skeletal Population: Demographic and Methodological Aspects," *American Journal of Biological Anthropology* 19, no. 3 (September 1961): 237–244.

6   "Historical Estimates of World Population," United States Census Bureau, n.d., https://www.census.gov/data/tables/time-series/demo/international-programs/historical-est-worldpop.html.

7   United Nations Secretariat, Department of Economic and Social Affairs, Population Division, *The World at Six Billion* (New York: United Nations, 1999).

8   United Nations Secretariat, Department of Economic and Social Affairs, Population Division, *The World at Six Billion*.

9   "Historical Estimates of World Population," United States Census Bureau, n.d., https://www.census.gov/data/tables/time-series/demo/international-programs/historical-est-worldpop.html.

10   Yuval Noah Harari, *Sapiens: A Brief History of Humankind* (New York: Harper Collins Publishers, 2015).

11   Harari, *Sapiens*.

12   Mark Maslin and Simon Lewis, "Why the Anthropocene Began with European Colonisation, Mass Slavery and the 'Great Dying' of the 16th Century," The Conversation, June 25, 2020, https://theconversation.com/why-the-anthropocene-began-with-european-colonisation-mass-slavery-and-the-great-dying-of-the-16th-century-140661.

13   Marian L. Tupy and Gale L. Pooley, *Superabundance: The Story of Population Growth, Innovation, and Human Flourishing on an Infinitely Bountiful Planet* (Washington, DC: Cato Institute, 2022).

14   "Historical Estimates of World Population," United States Census Bureau, n.d., https://www.census.gov/data/tables/time-series/demo/international-programs/historical-est-worldpop.html.

15   Thomas Robert Malthus, *An Essay on the Principle of Population* (London: J Johnson, 1798).

16 Malthus, *Essay.*

17 Malthus, *Essay.*

18 Marian L. Tupy and Gale L. Pooley, *Superabundance: The Story of Population Growth, Innovation, and Human Flourishing on an Infinitely Bountiful Planet* (Washington, DC: Cato Institute, 2022).

19 Francis Galton, *Essays in Eugenics by Francis Galton*, Sir Francis Galton FRS, 1909, https://galton.org/cgi-bin/searchImages/galton/search/books/essays-on-eugenics/pages/essays-eugenics_0049.htm.

20 Fred Pearce, *The Coming Population Crash: and Our Planet's Surprising Future* (Boston: Beacon Press, 2010).

21 Pearce, *Coming.*

22 David Saldana, "What Is White Replacement Theory—and How Is It Fueling Racist Attacks?," Reader's Digest, June 7, 2022, https://www.rd.com/article/white-replacement-theory/.

23 "8 Billion and Growing: World Population Milestones throughout History," Population Connection, July 6, 2022, https://populationconnection.org/blog/world-population-milestones-throughout-history/.

24 Population Connection, "8 Billion and Growing."

25 National Security Agency, "NSSM 200: Implications of Worldwide Population Growth for U.S. Security and Overseas Interests (The Kissinger Report)," USAID, December 10, 1974, https://pdf.usaid.gov/pdf_docs/PCAAB500.pdf.

26 Fred Pearce, *The Coming Population Crash: and Our Planet's Surprising Future* (Boston: Beacon Press, 2010).

27 Sandra L. Colby and Jennifer M. Ortman, "The Baby Boom Cohort in the United States: 2012 to 2060," United States Census Bureau, May

2014, https://www.census.gov/content/dam/Census/library/publications/2014/demo/p25-1141.pdf.

28   "Fertility Rate, Total (Births per Woman)," World Bank, n.d., https://data.worldbank.org/indicator/SP.DYN.TFRT.IN?view=chart.

29   "Life Expectancy," Scientific American, May 13, 2002, https://www.scientificamerican.com/article/life-expectancy.

30   "Fertility Rate, Total (Births per Woman)," World Bank, n.d., https://data.worldbank.org/indicator/SP.DYN.TFRT.IN?view=chart.

31   Fairfield Osborn, *Our Plundered Planet* (New York: Little Brown, 1948).

32   Osborn, *Our Plundered Planet.*

33   William Vogt, *Road to Survival* (New York: W. Sloane Associates, 1948).

34   Hugh Moore, "The Population Bomb," 1954.

35   Moore, "The Population Bomb."

36   Paul R. Ehrlich, *The Population Bomb* (New York: Sierra Club/Ballantine Books, 1968).

37   Edward Goldsmith, *A Blueprint for Survival* (New York City: Penguin Books Ltd., 1973).

38   Damian Carrington, "Paul Ehrlich: 'Collapse of Civilisation Is a Near Certainty within Decades,'" Guardian, March 22, 2018, https://www.theguardian.com/cities/2018/mar/22/collapse-civilisation-near-certain-decades-population-bomb-paul-ehrlich.

39   Fred Pearce, *The Coming Population Crash: and Our Planet's Surprising Future* (Boston: Beacon Press, 2010).

40 Wajahat Ali, "The Case for Having Kids," comments, TED, 2019, https://www.ted.com/talks/wajahat_ali_the_case_ for_having_kids?fbclid=IwAR3Rk41Xrk0v64UFFu5iTDLr yoD-5sZrn7Rm4yb-u6JkJTNHsp_fz5aHQRU.

41 Fred Pearce, "The Real Green Revolution," *New Scientist*, December 13, 1997, https://www.newscientist.com/article/ mg15621126-800-the-real-green-revolution/.

Chapter 2

42 David Adam, "How Far Will Global Population Rise? Researchers Can't Agree," *Nature*, September 21, 2021, https://www.nature.com/ articles/d41586-021-02522-6.

43 Emil Vollset et al., "Fertility, Mortality, Migration, and Population Scenarios for 195 Countries and Territories from 2017 to 2011: A Forecasting Analysis for the Global Burden of Disease Study," *Lancet* 396, no. 10258 (2020): 1285–1306, https://www.thelancet.com/ journals/lancet/article/PIIS0140-6736(20)30677-2/fulltext.

44 Vollset et al., "Fertility."

45 Michael Herrmann, "The Global Population Will Soon Reach 8 Billion— Then What?" United Nations, July 11, 2022, https://www.un.org/en/ un-chronicle/global-population-will-soon-reach-8-billion-then-what.

46 "2022–23 Enrollment by Grade Report (District)," Massachusetts Department of Education, last updated December 1, 2022. https:// profiles.doe.mass.edu/statereport/enrollmentbygrade.aspx.

47 American Community Survey Table S0101 Hingham Town, United States Census Bureau, n.d., https://data.census.gov/table?q=PEPAGE &t=Age+and+Sex&g=0100000US_0400000US25_0500000US2502 3_0600000US2502330210&tid=ACSST1Y2019.S0101.

48   United States Census Bureau, American Community Survey.

49   Alex Macon, "What the New Census Numbers Tell Us about Dallas-Fort Worth's Growth," *D Magazine*, August 12, 2021, https://www.dmagazine.com/frontburner/2021/08/what-the-new-census-numbers-tell-us-about-dallas-fort-worths-growth/.

50   Mitchell Parton, "D-FW Builders Ramp Up Home Starts, Pushing to Keep Up with Demand," *Dallas Morning News*, April 21, 2022, https://www.dallasnews.com/business/real-estate/2022/04/11/d-fw-builders-ramp-up-home-starts-pushing-to-keep-up-with-demand/.

51   UN Population Division Data Portal, United Nations Population Division, 2022, https://population.un.org/dataportal/data/indicators/19/locations/156/start/1950/end/2022/table/pivotbylocation.

52   Drew Grover, "What Is the Demographic Transition Model?" Population Education, October 13, 2014, https://populationeducation.org/what-demographic-transition-model/.

53   "Demographic Dividend," United Nations Population Fund, n.d., https://www.unfpa.org/demographic-dividend#readmore-expand.

54   David Adam, "How Far Will Global Population Rise? Researchers Can't Agree," *Nature*, September 21, 2021, https://www.nature.com/articles/d41586-021-02522-6.

55   Adam, "Population Rise."

56   Darrell Bricker and John Ibbitson, *Empty Planet: The Shock of Global Population Decline* (New York: Crown Publishing, 2019).

57   Philip DeCicca and Harry Krashinsky, "The Effect of Education on Overall Fertility," National Bureau of Economic Research, December 2016, https://www.nber.org/papers/w23003.

58 Dakar and Kano, "The World's Peak Population May Be Smaller Than Expected," *Economist*, April 5, 2023, https://www.economist.com/middle-east-and-africa/2023/04/05/the-worlds-peak-population-may-be-smaller-than-expected.

59 Laurie DeRose and Lyman Stone, "More Work, Fewer Babies: What Does Workism Have to Do with Falling Fertility?" Institute for Family Studies, https://ifstudies.org/ifs-admin/resources/reports/ifs-workismreport-final-031721.pdf.

60 Jessica Grose, "Are Men the Overlooked Reason for Fertility Decline?" *New York Times*, February 15, 2023, https://www.nytimes.com/2023/02/15/opinion/fertility-decline.html.

61 Darrell Bricker and John Ibbitson, *Empty Planet: The Shock of Global Population Decline* (New York: Crown Publishing, 2019).

62 Dakar and Kano, "The World's Peak Population May Be Smaller Than Expected," *Economist*, April 5, 2023, https://www.economist.com/middle-east-and-africa/2023/04/05/the-worlds-peak-population-may-be-smaller-than-expected.

63 Darrell Bricker and John Ibbitson, *Empty Planet: The Shock of Global Population Decline* (New York: Crown Publishing, 2019).

64 "National Life Tables—Life Expectancy in the UK: 2018 to 2020," Office for National Statistics, September 23, 2021, https://www.ons.gov.uk/peoplepopulationandcommunity/birthsdeathsandmarriages/lifeexpectancies/bulletins/nationallifetablesunitedkingdom/2018to2020.

65 Maddison Erbabian, Austin Herrick, and Victoria Osorio, "The Decline in Fertility: The Role of Marriage and Education," Penn Wharton, July 8, 2022, https://budgetmodel.wharton.upenn.edu/issues/2022/7/8/decline-in-fertility-the-role-of-marriage-and-education.

66 Erbabian, Herrick, and Osorio, "The Decline in Fertility."

67 "Age at First Birth," USAID, n.d., https://www.data4impactproject. org/prh/family-planning/fertility/age-at-first-birth/.

68 Ellen Wiebe, Amanda Chalmers, and Holly Yager, "Delayed Motherhood: Understanding the Experiences of Women Older Than Age 33 Who Are Having Abortions but Plan to Become Mothers Later," *Canadian Family Physician* 58, no. 10 (2012): e588–e595, https:// www.ncbi.nlm.nih.gov/pmc/articles/PMC3470537/.

69 "Motherhood Deferred: U.S. Median Age for Giving Birth Hits 30," Associated Press, May 8, 2022, https://www.nbcnews.com/news/ motherhood-deferred-us-median-age-giving-birth-hits-30-rcna27827.

70 Vegard Skirbekk, "Fertility Trends by Social Status." *Demographic Research* 18, no. 5 (2008): 145–180, https://www.demographic-research.org/VOLUMES/VOL18/5/18-5.PDF.

71 Nicholas Eberstadt, "China's Collapsing Birth and Marriage Rates Reflect a People's Deep Pessimism," *Washington Post*, February 28, 2023, https://www.washingtonpost.com/opinions/2023/02/28/behind-china-collapse-birth-marriage-rates/?utm_campaign=wp_post_most&utm_medium=email&utm_source=newsletter&wpisrc=nl_most&carta-url=https%3A%2F%2Fs2.washingtonpost.com%2Fcar-ln-tr%2F3941b06%2F63ff88fe1b.

72 Melissa S. Kearney and Phillip B. Levine, "The Consequences and Causes of Declining US Fertility," The Aspen Economic Strategy Group, August 13, 2022, https://www.economicstrategygroup.org/ publication/kearney_levine/.

73 Amir Ali, "BC Has the Lowest Fertility Rate in Canada. Is the Cost of Housing to Blame?," Daily Hive, September 1, 2022, https://dailyhive. com/vancouver/bc-lowest-fertility-canada-housing.

74 "Average Undergraduate Tuition, Fees, Room, and Board Rates Charged for Full-Time Students in Degree-Granting Postsecondary Institutions, by Level and Control of Institution: Selected Years,

1963–64 Through 2020–21," Institute of Education Sciences National Center for Education Statistics, 2021, https://nces.ed.gov/programs/digest/d21/tables/dt21_330.10.asp.

75   Institute of Education Sciences National Center for Education Statistics. 2021. *Average Undergraduate Tuition, Fees, Room, and Board Rates Charged for Full-Time Students in Degree-Granting Postsecondary Institutions, by Level and Control of Institution: Selected Years, 1963-64 Through 2020-21.* https://nces.ed.gov/programs/digest/d21/tables/dt21_330.10.asp.

76   Michael Bar et al., "Why Did Rich Families Increase Their Fertility? Inequality and Marketization of Child Care," *Journal of Economic Growth* 23 (2018): 427–463.

77   Jonathan V. Last, *What to Expect When No One's Expecting: America's Coming Demographic Disaster* (New York: Encounter Books, 2013).

78   Gloria Goodale, "Behind the Falling US Birthrate: Too Much Student Debt to Afford Kids?" *New York Times*, January 30, 2013, https://www.nytimes.com/2018/07/05/upshot/americans-are-having-fewer-babies-they-told-us-why.html.

79   Jonathan V. Last, *What to Expect When No One's Expecting: America's Coming Demographic Disaster* (New York: Encounter Books, 2013).

80   Melissa S. Kearney and Phillip B. Levine, "The Consequences and Causes of Declining US Fertility," The Aspen Economic Strategy Group, August 13, 2022, https://www.economicstrategygroup.org/publication/kearney_levine/.

81   Claire Cain Miller, "Americans Are Having Fewer Babies. They Told Us Why," *New York Times*, July 5, 2018, https://www.nytimes.com/2018/07/05/upshot/americans-are-having-fewer-babies-they-told-us-why.html.

82 Jessica Grose, "Are Men the Overlooked Reason for Fertility Decline?" *New York Times*, February 15, 2023, https://www.nytimes.com/2023/02/15/opinion/fertility-decline.html.

83 Jonathan V. Last, *What to Expect When No One's Expecting: America's Coming Demographic Disaster* (New York: Encounter Books, 2013).

84 Adam M. Carrington, "Montesquieu's Warning about Our Childlessness," Law & Liberty, September 2, 2022, https://lawliberty.org/montesquieus-warning-about-our-childlessness/.

85 "United Nations Population Division," United Nations, n.d., https://www.un.org/development/desa/pd/.

86 "About United Nations Population Division," United Nations, n.d., https://www.un.org/development/desa/pd/content/about-the-un.

87 "World Population Prospects 2022," United Nations, 2022, https://www.un.org/development/desa/pd/sites/www.un.org.development.desa.pd/files/wpp2022_summary_of_results.pdf.

88 United Nations, "World Population Prospects 2022."

89 United Nations, "World Population Prospects 2022."

90 Max Roser and Lucas Rodés-Guirao, "Future Population Growth," Our World in Data, last revised November 2019, https://ourworldindata.org/future-population-growth.

91 Emil Vollset et al., "Fertility, Mortality, Migration, and Population Scenarios for 195 Countries and Territories from 2017 to 2011: A Forecasting Analysis for the Global Burden of Disease Study," *Lancet* 396, no. 10258 (2020): 1285–1306, https://www.thelancet.com/journals/lancet/article/PIIS0140-6736(20)30677-2/fulltext.

Chapter 3

92 Paul R. Ehrlich, *The Population Bomb* (New York: Sierra Club/Ballantine Books, 1968).

93 "The Early Years," The Norman Borlaug Heritage Foundation, n.d., https://www.normanborlaug.org/norman-borlaug-bio.

94 Norman Borlaug, "The Green Revolution, Peace, and Humanity," The Nobel Prize, December 11, 1970, https://www.nobelprize.org/prizes/peace/1970/borlaug/lecture/.

95 Russell P. Kaniuka, "History of Research at the US Department of Agriculture and Agricultural Research Service," USDA, last modified February 14, 2018, https://www.ars.usda.gov/oc/timeline/green/.

96 Hannah Ritchie, "Yield vs. Land Use: How the Green Revolution Enabled Us to Feed a Growing Population," Our World in Data, August 22, 2017, https://ourworldindata.org/yields-vs-land-use-how-has-the-world-produced-enough-food-for-a-growing-population.

97 Gordon Conway, *Doubly Green Revolution: Food for All in the Twenty-First Century* (London: Penguin UK, 1999).

98 Peter B. R. Hazell, "Green Revolution: Curse or Blessing?" International Food Policy Research Institute, 2002, https://people.forestry.oregonstate.edu/steve-strauss/sites/people.forestry.oregonstate.edu.steve-strauss/files/GreenRevo-Curse-or-Blessing-IFPRI.pdf.

99 Peter Hazell, "Think Again: The Green Revolution," Foreign Policy, September 22, 2009, https://foreignpolicy.com/2009/09/22/think-again-the-green-revolution/.

100 Fred Pearce, *The Coming Population Crash: and Our Planet's Surprising Future* (Boston: Beacon Press, 2010).

101 Peter B. R. Hazell, "Green Revolution: Curse or Blessing?" International Food Policy Research Institute, 2002, https://people.forestry. oregonstate.edu/steve-strauss/sites/people.forestry.oregonstate.edu. steve-strauss/files/GreenRevo-Curse-or-Blessing-IFPRI.pdf.

102 Norman Borlaug, "The Green Revolution, Peace, and Humanity," The Nobel Prize, December 11, 1970, https://www.nobelprize.org/prizes/ peace/1970/borlaug/lecture/.

103 Borlaug, "Green Revolution."

104 Fred Pearce, *The Coming Population Crash: and Our Planet's Surprising Future* (Boston: Beacon Press, 2010).

105 Fahd Kahn et al., "The Story of the Condom," *Indian Journal of Urology* 29, no. 1 (2012): 12–15. https://www.ncbi.nlm.nih.gov/pmc/articles/ PMC3649591/.

106 "Eugenics and Birth Control," PBS, n.d., https://www.pbs.org/wgbh/ americanexperience/features/pill-eugenics-and-birth-control/.

107 Alexander Sanger, "Eugenics, Race, and Margaret Sanger Revisited: Reproductive Freedom for All?" *Hypatia* 22 no. 2 (2007): 210–217, https://www.jstor.org/ stable/4640075?mag=margaret-sangers-eugenics-defense&seq=1.

108 "The Population Council," Rockefeller Brothers Fund, n.d., https:// www.rbf.org/about/our-history/timeline/population-council.

109 Fred Pearce, *The Coming Population Crash: and Our Planet's Surprising Future* (Boston: Beacon Press, 2010).

110 Phyllis Tilson Piotrow, *World Population Crisis: The United States Response* (New York: Praeger Publishers, 1973).

111 Fred Pearce, *The Coming Population Crash: and Our Planet's Surprising Future* (Boston: Beacon Press, 2010).

112 National Security Agency, "NSSM 200: Implications of Worldwide Population Growth for U.S. Security and Overseas Interests (The Kissinger Report)," USAID, December 10, 1974, https://pdf.usaid.gov/pdf_docs/PCAAB500.pdf.

113 Fred Pearce, *The Coming Population Crash: and Our Planet's Surprising Future* (Boston: Beacon Press, 2010).

114 Pearce, *The Coming Population Crash.*

115 Ajit Niranjan, "How Will a Decreasing Global Population Impact the Planet?," Deutsche Well, August 31, 2020, https://www.dw.com/en/overpopulation-climate-change-emissions/a-54725928.

116 Jason Leonard Finkle and C. Alison McIntosh, *The New Politics of Population: Conflict and Consensus in Family Planning* (New York City: Population Council, 1994).

117 "Total Population, CBR, CDR, NIR and TFR of China (1949-2000)," *China Daily* August 20, 2010, http://www.chinadaily.com.cn/china/2010census/2010-08/20/content_11182379.htm.

118 Malcolm Potts, "China's One Child Policy," *BMJ* 333, no. 7564 (2006): 361–362, https://www.ncbi.nlm.nih.gov/pmc/articles/PMC1550444/.

119 Laura Fitzpatrick, "A Brief History of China's One-Child Policy," *TIME*, July 27, 2009, http://content.time.com/time/world/article/0,8599,1912861,00.html.

120 Fitzpatrick, "One-Child Policy."

121 Frank Dikötter, *Mao's Great Famine* (London: Walker & Company, 2010).

122 "China's Population: Issues and Trends in China's Demographic History," Weatherhead East Asian Institute, Columbia University, n.d., http://afe.easia.columbia.edu/special/china_1950_population.htm.

123 UN Population Division Data Portal, United Nations Population Division, 2022, https://population.un.org/dataportal/data/indicators/19/locations/156/start/1950/end/2022/table/pivotbylocation.

124 "China Population 1950-2022," Macrotrends, n.d., https://www.macrotrends.net/countries/CHN/china/population.

125 Malcolm Potts, "China's One Child Policy," *BMJ* 333, no. 7564 (2006): 361–362, https://www.ncbi.nlm.nih.gov/pmc/articles/PMC1550444/.

126 Fred Pearce, *The Coming Population Crash: and Our Planet's Surprising Future* (Boston: Beacon Press, 2010).

127 Jonathan V. Last, *What to Expect When No One's Expecting: America's Coming Demographic Disaster* (New York: Encounter Books, 2013).

128 Marian L. Tupy and Gale L. Pooley, *Superabundance: The Story of Population Growth, Innovation, and Human Flourishing on an Infinitely Bountiful Planet* (Washington, DC: Cato Institute, 2022).

129 Jonathan V. Last, *What to Expect When No One's Expecting: America's Coming Demographic Disaster* (New York: Encounter Books, 2013).

130 Darrell Bricker and John Ibbitson, *Empty Planet: The Shock of Global Population Decline* (New York: Crown Publishing, 2019).

131 UN Population Division Data Portal, United Nations Population Division, 2022, https://population.un.org/dataportal/data/indicators/19/locations/156/start/1950/end/2022/table/pivotbylocation.

132 Data Portal, United Nations Population Division.

133 Ken Moritsugu, "China Records 1st Population Fall in Decades as Births Drop," January 17, 2023, *Chicago Tribune*, https://www.chicagotribune.com/nation-world/ct-aud-nw-china-population-decline-20230117-5nxyroz6tng2lmvzofuzyui53q-story.html.

134 Nicole Hong and Zixu Wang, "Desperate for Babies, China Races to Undo an Era of Birth Limits. Is It Too Late?" *New York Times*, February 26, 2023, https://www.nytimes.com/2023/02/26/world/asia/china-birth-rate.html.

135 Nicholas Eberstadt, "China's Collapsing Birth and Marriage Rates Reflect a People's Deep Pessimism," *Washington Post*, February 28, 2023, https://www.washingtonpost.com/opinions/2023/02/28/behind-china-collapse-birth-marriage-rates/?utm_campaign=wp_post_most&utm_medium=email&utm_source=newsletter&wpisrc=nl_most&carta-url=https%3A%2F%2Fs2.washingtonpost.com%2Fcar-ln-tr%2F3941b06%2F63ff88fe1b.

136 Marian L. Tupy and Gale L. Pooley, *Superabundance: The Story of Population Growth, Innovation, and Human Flourishing on an Infinitely Bountiful Planet* (Washington, DC: Cato Institute, 2022).

137 Tupy and Pooley, *Superabundance*.

138 Tupy and Pooley, *Superabundance*.

139 Tupy and Pooley, *Superabundance*.

140 Tupy and Pooley, *Superabundance*.

141 Tupy and Pooley, *Superabundance*.

Chapter 4

142 UN Population Division Data Portal, United Nations Population Division, 2022, https://population.un.org/dataportal/data/indicators/19/locations/156/start/1950/end/2022/table/pivotbylocation.

143 Spencer Bokat-Lindell, "U.S. Population Growth Has Flatline. Is That So Bad?" *New York Times*, September 14, 2022, https://www.nytimes.com/2022/09/14/opinion/population-birthrate-decline.html.

144 Hafiz T. A. Khan and Wolfgang Lutz, "How Well Did Past UN Population Projections Anticipate Demographic Trends in Six Southeast Asia Countries?," Oxford Institute of Population Ageing, November 2007, https://www.ageing.ox.ac.uk/files/workingpaper_507.pdf.

145 UN Population Division Data Portal, United Nations Population Division, 2022, https://population.un.org/dataportal/data/indicators/19/locations/156/start/1950/end/2022/table/pivotbylocation.

146 Darrell Bricker and John Ibbitson, *Empty Planet: The Shock of Global Population Decline* (New York: Crown Publishing, 2019).

147 Emil Vollset et al., "Fertility, Mortality, Migration, and Population Scenarios for 195 Countries and Territories from 2017 to 2011: A Forecasting Analysis for the Global Burden of Disease Study," *Lancet* 396, no. 10258 (2020): 1285–1306, https://www.thelancet.com/journals/lancet/article/PIIS0140-6736(20)30677-2/fulltext.

148 Jonathan V. Last, *What to Expect When No One's Expecting: America's Coming Demographic Disaster* (New York: Encounter Books, 2013).

149 UN Population Division Data Portal, United Nations Population Division, 2022, https://population.un.org/dataportal/

data/indicators/19/locations/156/start/1950/end/2022/table/
pivotbylocation.

150 Data Portal, United Nations Population Division.

151 "The Impact of Population Momentum on Future Population Growth,"
United Nations Population Division, October 2017, https://www.
un.org/en/development/desa/population/publications/pdf/popfacts/
PopFacts_2017-4.pdf.

152   United Nations Population Division, "Future Population Growth."

153 Jonathan V. Last, *What to Expect When No One's Expecting: America's
Coming Demographic Disaster* (New York: Encounter Books, 2013).

154 David Adam, "How Far Will Global Population Rise? Researchers
Can't Agree," *Nature*, September 21, 2021, https://www.nature.com/
articles/d41586-021-02522-6.

155 Wolfgang Lutz et al., eds., "Demographic and Human Capital Scenarios
for the 21st Century: 2018 Assessment for 201 Countries," European
Commission, 2018.

156 Lutz et al., "Demographic."

157 Lutz et al., "Demographic."

158 "The 17 Goals," United Nations Department of Economic and Social
Affairs, n.d., https://sdgs.un.org/goals.

159 Max Roser and Lucas Rodés-Guirao, "Future Population Growth,"
2019, https://ourworldindata.org/future-population-growth.

160 Emil Vollset et al., "Fertility, Mortality, Migration, and Population
Scenarios for 195 Countries and Territories from 2017 to 2011: A
Forecasting Analysis for the Global Burden of Disease Study," *Lancet*

396, no. 10258 (2020): 1285–1306, https://www.thelancet.com/journals/lancet/article/PIIS0140-6736(20)30677-2/fulltext.

161   Vollset et al., "Fertility."

162   Vollset et al., "Fertility."

163   UN Population Division Data Portal, United Nations Population Division, 2022, https://population.un.org/dataportal/data/indicators/19/locations/156/start/1950/end/2022/table/pivotbylocation.

164   Wolfgang Lutz et al., eds., "Demographic and Human Capital Scenarios for the 21st Century: 2018 Assessment for 201 Countries," European Commission, 2018.

165   Emil Vollset et al., "Fertility, Mortality, Migration, and Population Scenarios for 195 Countries and Territories from 2017 to 2011: A Forecasting Analysis for the Global Burden of Disease Study," *Lancet* 396, no. 10258 (2020): 1285–1306, https://www.thelancet.com/journals/lancet/article/PIIS0140-6736(20)30677-2/fulltext.

166   "WHO Coronavirus (COVID-19) Dashboard," World Health Organization, January 31, 2023, https://covid19.who.int/.

167   David Adam, "How Far Will Global Population Rise? Researchers Can't Agree," *Nature*, September 21, 2021, https://www.nature.com/articles/d41586-021-02522-6.

168   Nectar Gan and Steve George, "China's Birthrate Just Hit Another Record Low. But the Worst Is Yet to Come," CNN, December 1, 2021, https://www.cnn.com/2021/12/01/china/china-birthrate-2020-mic-intl-hnk/index.html.

169   Alexandra Stevenson and Zixu Wang, "China's Population Falls, Heralding a Demographic Crisis," *New York Times*, January 16, 2023,

https://www.nytimes.com/2023/01/16/business/china-birth-rate.
html?smid=em-share.

170 Stevenson and Wang, "China's Population Falls."

171 David Adam, "How Far Will Global Population Rise? Researchers
Can't Agree," *Nature*, September 21, 2021, https://www.nature.com/
articles/d41586-021-02522-6.

172 Adam, "Population Rise."

173 "The Economics of Falling Populations," *Economist*, March 27, 2021,
https://www.economist.com/finance-and-economics/2021/03/27/
the-economics-of-falling-populations.

174 "World Population Prospects 2022: Summary of Results," United
Nations Department of Economic and Social Affairs, July 2022,
https://www.un.org/development/desa/pd/sites/www.un.org.develop-
ment.desa.pd/files/undesa_pd_2022_wpp_key-messages.pdf.

175 Statistics in this section are from 2021 UNPD data unless otherwise
indicated. (See https://population.un.org/wpp/Download/Standard/
MostUsed/.)

176 Ibid.

177 Nicholas Eberstadt, "Can America Cope with Demographic Decline?,"
American Enterprise Institute, October 6, 2021, https://www.aei.org/
articles/can-america-cope-with-demographic-decline/.

178 Darrell Bricker and John Ibbitson, *Empty Planet: The Shock of Global
Population Decline* (New York: Crown Publishing, 2019).

179 "South Korea's World Lowest Fertility Rate Drops Again," Reuters,
February 22, 2023, https://www.reuters.com/world/asia-pacific/
south-koreas-world-lowest-fertility-rate-drops-again-2023-02-22/.

180 Jessica Grose, "If We Want More Babies, Our 'Profoundly Anti-Family' System Needs an Overhaul," *New York Times*, March 8, 2023, https://www.nytimes.com/2023/03/08/opinion/birth-rate.html.

181 Nicholas Eberstadt, "China's Collapsing Birth and Marriage Rates Reflect a People's Deep Pessimism," *Washington Post*, February 28, 2023, https://www.washingtonpost.com/opinions/2023/02/28/behind-china-collapse-birth-marriage-rates/?utm_campaign=wp_post_most&utm_medium=email&utm_source=newsletter&wpisrc=nl_most&carta-url=https%3A%2F%2Fs2.washingtonpost.com%2Fcar-ln-tr%2F3941b06%2F63ff88fe1b.

182 Michael Herrmann, "The Global Population Will Soon Reach 8 Billion—Then What?" United Nations, July 11, 2022, https://www.un.org/en/un-chronicle/global-population-will-soon-reach-8-billion-then-what.

183 Jonathan V. Last, *What to Expect When No One's Expecting: America's Coming Demographic Disaster* (New York: Encounter Books, 2013).

184 Dakar and Kano, "The World's Peak Population May Be Smaller Than Expected," *Economist*, April 5, 2023, https://www.economist.com/middle-east-and-africa/2023/04/05/the-worlds-peak-population-may-be-smaller-than-expected.

185 Dakar and Kano, "The World's Peak Population."

186 Christian Shepherd, "China's First Population Decline in 60 Years Sounds Demographic Alarm," *Washington Post*, January 17, 2023, https://www.washingtonpost.com/world/2023/01/17/china-population-shrinking-decline-crisis/?utm_campaign=wp_post_most&utm_medium=email&utm_source=newsletter&wpisrc=nl_most&carta-url=https%3A%2F%2Fs2.washingtonpost.com%2Fcar-ln-tr%2F38df9ca%2F63c6d31def9bf6.

187 Emil Vollset et al., "Fertility, Mortality, Migration, and Population Scenarios for 195 Countries and Territories from 2017 to 2011: A Forecasting Analysis for the Global Burden of Disease Study," *Lancet*

396, no. 10258 (2020): 1285–1306, https://www.thelancet.com/journals/lancet/article/PIIS0140-6736(20)30677-2/fulltext.

188 Christian Shepherd, "China's First Population Decline in 60 Years Sounds Demographic Alarm," *Washington Post*, January 17, 2023, https://www.washingtonpost.com/world/2023/01/17/china-population-shrinking-decline-crisis/?utm_campaign=wp_post_most&utm_medium=email&utm_source=newsletter&wpisrc=nl_most&carta-url=https%3A%2F%2Fs2.washingtonpost.com%2Fcar-ln-tr%2F38df9ca%2F63c6d31def9bf6.

189 Jonathan V. Last, *What to Expect When No One's Expecting: America's Coming Demographic Disaster* (New York: Encounter Books, 2013).

190 Brent Peabody., "Russia Doesn't Have the Demographics for War," Foreign Policy, January 2, 2022, https://foreignpolicy.com/2022/01/03/russia-demography-birthrate-decline-ukraine/.

191 "World Population Prospects 2022: Summary of Results," United Nations Department of Economic and Social Affairs, July 2022, https://www.un.org/development/desa/pd/sites/www.un.org.development.desa.pd/files/undesa_pd_2022_wpp_key-messages.pdf.

192 Elissa Nadworny, "Ukraine's Birth Rate Was Already Dangerously Low. Then War Broke Out," NPR, February 22, 2023, https://www.npr.org/2023/02/22/1155943055/ukraine-low-birth-rate-russia-war.

193 Nicholas Eberstadt, "Can America Cope with Demographic Decline?," American Enterprise Institute, October 6, 2021, https://www.aei.org/articles/can-america-cope-with-demographic-decline/.

194 Emil Vollset et al., "Fertility, Mortality, Migration, and Population Scenarios for 195 Countries and Territories from 2017 to 2011: A Forecasting Analysis for the Global Burden of Disease Study," *Lancet* 396, no. 10258 (2020): 1285–1306, https://www.thelancet.com/journals/lancet/article/PIIS0140-6736(20)30677-2/fulltext.

195 Fred Pearce, *The Coming Population Crash: and Our Planet's Surprising Future* (Boston: Beacon Press, 2010).

196 Peter McDonald, "Low Fertility and the State: The Efficacy of Policy," *Population and Development Review* 32, no. 3 (2006): 485–501.

197 McDonald, "Low Fertility and the State."

198 Darrell Bricker and John Ibbitson, *Empty Planet: The Shock of Global Population Decline* (New York: Crown Publishing, 2019).

199 Pew Research Center, "Young Adults around the World Are Less Religious by Several Measures" (Washington DC: Pew Research Center, 2018).

200 Nicholas Eberstadt, "Can America Cope with Demographic Decline?," American Enterprise Institute, October 6, 2021, https://www.aei.org/articles/can-america-cope-with-demographic-decline/.

201 Lyman Stone, "Baby Blues: How to Face the Church's Growing Fertility Crisis," Christianity Today, August 8, 2022, https://www.christianity-today.com/ct/2022/august-web-only/birth-rates-church-attendance-decline-fertility-crisis.html.

202 Darrell Bricker and John Ibbitson, *Empty Planet: The Shock of Global Population Decline* (New York: Crown Publishing, 2019).

203 Fred Pearce, *The Coming Population Crash: and Our Planet's Surprising Future* (Boston: Beacon Press, 2010).

204 Darrell Bricker and John Ibbitson, *Empty Planet: The Shock of Global Population Decline* (New York: Crown Publishing, 2019).

205 "68% of the World Population Projected to Live in Urban Areas by 2050, Says UN," United Nations Department of Economic and Social Affairs, May 16, 2018, https://www.un.org/development/desa/

en/news/population/2018-revision-of-world-urbanization-prospects. html.

206 United Nations Department of Economic and Social Affairs, "Urban Areas."

207 Darrell Bricker and John Ibbitson, *Empty Planet: The Shock of Global Population Decline* (New York: Crown Publishing, 2019).

208 Daniel F. Rundle, "Will Many Developing Countries Get Old Before They Get Rich?," CSIS, March 31, 2020, https://www.csis.org/analysis/ will-many-developing-countries-get-old-they-get-rich.

209 Peter McDonald, "Low Fertility Not Politically Sustainable," Population Reference Bureau, September 1, 2001, https://www.prb.org/ resources/low-fertility-not-politically-sustainable/.

210 Emil Vollset et al., "Fertility, Mortality, Migration, and Population Scenarios for 195 Countries and Territories from 2017 to 2011: A Forecasting Analysis for the Global Burden of Disease Study," *Lancet* 396, no. 10258 (2020): 1285–1306, https://www.thelancet.com/ journals/lancet/article/PIIS0140-6736(20)30677-2/fulltext.

Chapter 5

211 Emil Vollset et al., "Fertility, Mortality, Migration, and Population Scenarios for 195 Countries and Territories from 2017 to 2011: A Forecasting Analysis for the Global Burden of Disease Study," *Lancet* 396, no. 10258 (2020): 1285–1306, https://www.thelancet.com/ journals/lancet/article/PIIS0140-6736(20)30677-2/fulltext.

212 Richard Betts, "Met Office: Atmospheric CO2 Now Hitting 50% Higher Than Pre-Industrial Levels," World Economic Forum, March 22, 2021, https://www.weforum.org/agenda/2021/03/met-office- atmospheric-co2-industrial-levels-environment-climate-change/.

213 "Climate Change and Population," Union of Concerned Scientists, November 9, 2021, https://www.ucsusa.org/resources/climate-change-and-population.

214 Sophie Berger and Sarah Connors, eds., "Frequently Asked Questions," IPCC, n.d., https://www.ipcc.ch/report/ar6/wg1/downloads/faqs/IPCC_AR6_WGI_FAQs_Compiled.pdf.

215 Gregory Casey and Oded Galor, "Is Faster Economic Growth Compatible with Reductions in Carbon Emissions? The Role of Diminished Population Growth," *Environmental Research Letters* 12 no. 1 (2017), https://iopscience.iop.org/article/10.1088/1748-9326/12/1/014003/pdf.

216 Seth Wynes and Kimberly A. Nicholas, "The Climate Mitigation Gap: Education and Government Recommendations Miss the Most Effective Individual Actions," *Environmental Research Letters* (2017), https://iopscience.iop.org/article/10.1088/1748-9326/aa7541/pdf.

217 Matthew Schneider-Mayerson and Leong Kit Ling, "Eco-Reproductive Concerns in the Age of Climate Change," *Climatic Change* 163, no. 1007–1023 (2020). https://link.springer.com/article/10.1007/s10584-020-02923-y.

218 Sam Shead, "Climate Change Is Making People Think Twice About Having Children," CNBC, August 12, 2021, https://www.cnbc.com/2021/08/12/climate-change-is-making-people-think-twice-about-having-children.html.

219 Qin Li et al., "Association between Exposure to Airborne Particulate Matter Less Than 2.5 μm and Human Fecundity in China," *Environment International* 146, no. 106231 (January).

220 "Climate Change and Population," Union of Concerned Scientists, November 9, 2021, https://www.ucsusa.org/resources/climate-change-and-population.

221 Hannah Ritchie and Max Roser, "CO2 Emissions," Our World in Data, 2020, https://ourworldindata.org/co2-emissions.

222 Tim Gore, "Confronting Carbon Inequality: Putting Climate Justice at the Heart of the COVID-19 Recovery," Nairobi: Oxfam International, 2020, https://oxfamilibrary.openrepository.com/bitstream/handle/10546/621052/mb-confronting-carbon-inequality-210920-en.pdf.

223 Hannah Ritchie and Max Roser, "CO2 Emissions," Our World in Data, 2020, https://ourworldindata.org/co2-emissions.

224 Melissa S. Kearney and Phillip B. Levine, "The Consequences and Causes of Declining US Fertility," The Aspen Economic Strategy Group, August 13, 2022, https://www.economicstrategygroup.org/publication/kearney_levine/.

225 "Beyond GDP: Measuring Progress, Wealth and Wellbeing," European Commission, Global Footprint Network, 2018, https://ec.europa.eu/environment/beyond_gdp/download/factsheets/EcoF_new_template_2018-11-05_updated2.pdf.

226 "Ecological Footprint per Person," Global Footprint Network, 2018, https://data.footprintnetwork.org/?_ga=2.164104442.430807621.1658935934-192728006.1658935934#/.

227 Paul Krugman, "Learning to Live with Low Fertility," *New York Times*, May 17, 2021, https://www.nytimes.com/2021/05/17/opinion/low-population-growth-economy-inflation.html.

228 "The Productivity-Pay Gap," Economic Policy Institute, August, 2021, https://www.epi.org/productivity-pay-gap/.

229 Chancel et al., "World Inequality Report 2020," World Inequality Lab, 2022, https://wir2022.wid.world/www-site/uploads/2022/01/Summary_WorldInequalityReport2022_English.pdf.

230 Lili Pike, "The End of China's Population Boom Has Arrived. How Will the Country's Changing Demographics Shape Its Future?" The Messenger, July 12, 2022, https://www.grid.news/story/ global/2022/07/12/the-end-of-chinas-population-boom-has-arrived-how-will-the-countrys-changing-demographics-shape-its-future/.

231 Pike, "Population Boom."

232 "Eastern Europe's Workers Are Emigrating, but Its Pensioners Are Staying," Economist, January 19, 2017, https://www.economist.com/europe/2017/01/19/ eastern-europes-workers-are-emigrating-but-its-pensioners-are-staying.

233 United Nations Population Fund, "Shrinking Populations in Eastern Europe," UNFPA, n.d., https://eeca.unfpa.org/sites/default/files/ pub-pdf/Shrinking%20population_low%20fertility%20QA.pdf.

234 Charles Goodhart and Manoj Pradhan, *The Great Demographic Reversal: Ageing Societies, Waning Inequality, and an Inflation Revival* (London: Springer Nature, 2020).

235 Dakar and Kano, "The World's Peak Population May Be Smaller Than Expected," *Economist*, April 5, 2023, https:// www.economist.com/middle-east-and-africa/2023/04/05/ the-worlds-peak-population-may-be-smaller-than-expected.

236 Gina M. Raimondo, "Remarks by U.S. Secretary of Commerce Gina Raimondo: The CHIPS Act and a Long-term Vision for America's Technological Leadership," Law Firm Chronicle, February 23, 2023, https://www.lawfirmchronicle.com/2023/02/remarks-by-u-s-secre-tary-of-commerce-gina-raimondo-the-chips-act-and-a-long-term-vision-for-americas-technological-leadership/.

Chapter 6

237 Carmen Ang, "Mapped: Each Region's Median Age Since 1950," Visual Capitalist, 2020, https://www.visualcapitalist.com/median-age-changes-since-1950/.

238 "Age Dependency Ratio, Old (% of Working-Age Population)," Our World in Data, n.d., https://ourworldindata.org/search?q=old+age+dependency+ratio.

239 "Life Expectancy, 1770 to 2021," Our World in Data, n.d., https://ourworldindata.org/grapher/life-expectancy.

240 Peter Diamandis, "3 Amazing Longevity Companies," 2018, https://peterdiamandis.tumblr.com/post/165728301998/3-amazing-longevity-companies.

241 M. Szmigiera, "Projected Global Median Age from 1950 to 2100," Statista, 2022, https://www.statista.com/statistics/672669/projected-global-median-age/#:~:text=Projected%20global%20median%20age%201950-2100%20Published%20by%20M.,is%20projected%20to%20be%2041.9%20years%20of%20age.

242 "Median Age, 1950 to 2100," Our World in Data, 2022, https://ourworldindata.org/grapher/median-age.

243 "Median Age by State 2023," World Population Review, 2023, https://worldpopulationreview.com/state-rankings/median-age-by-state.

244 "Age Dependency Ratio, Old (% of Working-Age Population), Our World in Data, n.d., https://ourworldindata.org/search?q=old+age+dependency+ratio.

245 "World Population Prospects: The 2017 Revision," US Census Bureau, Population Division and United Nations Population Division, 2018.

246 "The World's Peak Population May Be Smaller Than Expected," *Economist*, April 5, 2023, https://www.economist.com/middle-east-and-africa/2023/04/05/the-worlds-peak-population-may-be-smaller-than-expected.

247 "World Population Prospects: The 2017 Revision," US Census Bureau, Population Division and United Nations Population Division, 2018.

248 Victor Reklaitis, "'We Need More People,' Says Fed's Powell. What Does That Mean for Immigration Reform?," MarketWatch, January 11, 2023, https://www.marketwatch.com/story/we-need-more-people-says-feds-powell-but-what-does-that-mean-for-immigration-reform-11671724198.

249 "Working Age Population: Aged 15–64: All Persons for the European Union," Federal Reserve Bank of St. Louis, April 17, 2020, https://fred.stlouisfed.org/series/LFWA64TTEUQ647N.

250 Lili Pike, "The End of China's Population Boom Has Arrived. How Will the Country's Changing Demographics Shape Its Future?" The Messenger, July 12, 2022, https://www.grid.news/story/global/2022/07/12/the-end-of-chinas-population-boom-has-arrived-how-will-the-countrys-changing-demographics-shape-its-future/.

251 Emil Vollset et al., "Fertility, Mortality, Migration, and Population Scenarios for 195 Countries and Territories from 2017 to 2011: A Forecasting Analysis for the Global Burden of Disease Study," *Lancet* 396, no. 10258 (2020): 1285–1306, https://www.thelancet.com/journals/lancet/article/PIIS0140-6736(20)30677-2/fulltext.

252 Charles Goodhart and Manoj Pradhan, *The Great Demographic Reversal: Ageing Societies, Waning Inequality, and an Inflation Revival* (London: Springer Nature, 2020).

253 Warren E. Buffett, "Letter to Shareholders of Berkshire Hathaway, Inc.," February 28, 2005, Berkshire Hathaway Inc., https://www.berkshirehathaway.com/letters/2004ltr.pdf.

254 Paul Krugman, "The Problem(s) with China's Population Drop," *New York Times*, January 17, 2023, https://www.nytimes.com/2023/01/17/opinion/china-population-economy.html.

255 Daniel F. Rundle, "Will Many Developing Countries Get Old Before They Get Rich?," CSIS, March 31, 2020, https://www.csis.org/analysis/will-many-developing-countries-get-old-they-get-rich.

256 Marc Freedman, *The Big Shift: Navigating the New Stage Beyond Midlife* (New York: PublicAffairs, 2011).

257 Marian L. Tupy and Gale L. Pooley, *Superabundance: The Story of Population Growth, Innovation, and Human Flourishing on an Infinitely Bountiful Planet* (Washington, DC: Cato Institute, 2022).

258 Burkhard Heer, Vito Polito, and Michael R. Wickens, "Population Aging, Social Security and Fiscal Limits," *CESifo Network*, 2018, https://www.cesifo.org/DocDL/cesifo1_wp7121.pdf#:~:text=Population%20Aging%2C%20Social%20Security%20and%20Fiscal%20Limits%20Abstract,limit%20to%20the%20real%20value%20of%20tax%20revenues.

259 Cecelia Rouse et al., "Life after Default," 2021, https://www.whitehouse.gov/cea/written-materials/2021/10/06/life-after-default/.

260 Neil Howe and Richard Jackson, "Global Aging and the Crisis of the 2020s," *Current History* 110, no. 732(2011): 20–25.

261 Jonathan V. Last, *What to Expect When No One's Expecting: America's Coming Demographic Disaster* (New York: Encounter Books, 2013).

262 Howe, Neil, and Richard Jackson. 2011. "Global Aging and the Crisis of the 2020s." *Current History* 110 (732): 20-25.

263 Charles Goodhart and Manoj Pradhan, *The Great Demographic Reversal: Ageing Societies, Waning Inequality, and an Inflation Revival* (London: Springer Nature, 2020).

264 Justin Nobel, "Japan's 'Lonely Deaths': A Business Opportunity," *TIME*, 2010, http://content.time.com/time/world/article/0,8599,1976952,00.html.

265 Jessica Grose, "'It's Pretty Brutal': The Sandwich Generation Pays a Price," *New York Times*, 2020, https://www.nytimes.com/2020/02/11/parenting/sandwich-generation-costs.html.

266 Darrell Bricker and John Ibbitson, *Empty Planet: The Shock of Global Population Decline* (New York: Crown Publishing, 2019).

267 Michael Balter, "The Baby Deficit," *Science* (2006.): 1894–1897, https://www.science.org/doi/10.1126/science.312.5782.1894.

268 Trent MacNamara, "Liberal Societies Have Dangerously Low Birth Rates," *Atlantic*, March 26, 2019, https://www.theatlantic.com/ideas/archive/2019/03/underpopulation-problem/585568/.

269 Marian L. Tupy and Gale L. Pooley, *Superabundance: The Story of Population Growth, Innovation, and Human Flourishing on an Infinitely Bountiful Planet* (Washington, DC: Cato Institute, 2022).

Chapter 7

270 Rick Gladstone, "World Population Could Peak Decades Ahead of U.N. Forecast, Study Asserts," *New York Times*, July 14, 2020, https://www.nytimes.com/2020/07/14/world/americas/global-population-trends.html#:~:text=The%20study%2C%20published%20in%20The%20Lancet%2C%20said%20an,shrink%20by%20more%20than%2050%20percent%20by%202100.?msclkid=967b02e6bcef11ecb74f365ff65ff4f4.

271 Darrell Bricker and John Ibbitson, *Empty Planet: The Shock of Global Population Decline* (New York: Crown Publishing, 2019).

272 Emil Vollset et al., "Fertility, Mortality, Migration, and Population Scenarios for 195 Countries and Territories from 2017 to 2011: A Forecasting Analysis for the Global Burden of Disease Study," *Lancet* 396, no. 10258 (2020): 1285–1306, https://www.thelancet.com/journals/lancet/article/PIIS0140-6736(20)30677-2/fulltext.

273 Melissa S. Kearney and Phillip B. Levine, "The Consequences and Causes of Declining US Fertility," The Aspen Economic Strategy Group, August 13, 2022, https://www.economicstrategygroup.org/publication/kearney_levine/.

274 Wajahat Ali, "The Case for Having Kids," comments, TED, 2019, https://www.ted.com/talks/wajahat_ali_the_case_for_having_kids?fbclid=IwAR3Rk41Xrk0v64UFFu5iTDLr yoD-5sZrn7Rm4yb-u6JkJTNHsp_fz5aHQRU.

275 United Nations Population Fund, "Shrinking Populations in Eastern Europe," UNFPA, n.d., https://eeca.unfpa.org/sites/default/files/pub-pdf/Shrinking%20population_low%20fertility%20QA.pdf.

276 Jeff Grabmeier, "Falling Birth Rate Not Due to Less Desire to Have Children," Ohio State News, January 12, 2023, https://news.osu.edu/falling-birth-rate-not-due-to-less-desire-to-have-children/.

277 Brady E. Hamilton, Joyce A. Martin, and Michelle J. K. Osterman, "Births: Provisional Data for 2021," Centers for Disease Control and Prevention, May 2022, https://www.cdc.gov/nchs/data/vsrr/vsrr020.pdf.

278 David G. Smith and W. Brad Johnson, "Gender Equity Starts in the Home," May 4, 2020, *Harvard Business Review*, https://hbr.org/2020/05/gender-equity-starts-in-the-home.

279 Jonathan V. Last, *What to Expect When No One's Expecting: America's Coming Demographic Disaster* (New York: Encounter Books, 2013).

280 "U.S. Pet Ownership Statistics," American Veterinary Medical Association. 2017–2018, https://www.avma.org/resources-tools/reports-statistics/us-pet-ownership-statistics#formulas.

281 "POP1 Child Population: Number of Children (in Millions) Ages 0–17 in the United States by Age, 1950–2021 and Projected 2022–2050," Child Stats, n.d., https://www.childstats.gov/americaschildren/tables/pop1.asp.

282 Peter McDonald, "Low Fertility and the State: The Efficacy of Policy," *Population and Development Review* 32, no. 3 (2006): 485–501.

283 McDonald, "Low Fertility and the State."

284 United Nations Population Fund, "Shrinking Populations in Eastern Europe," UNFPA, n.d., https://eeca.unfpa.org/sites/default/files/pub-pdf/Shrinking%20population_low%20fertility%20QA.pdf.

285 Kathleen Romig and Kathleen Bryant, "A National Paid Leave Program Would Help Workers, Families," April 27, 2021, https://www.cbpp.org/research/economy/a-national-paid-leave-program-would-help-workers-families.

286 Barbara Janta and Katherine Stewart, "Use It or Lose It—Why Taking Parental Leave Is So Important for Fathers," March 4, 2019, https://www.rand.org/blog/2019/03/use-it-or-lose-it-why-taking-parental-leave-is-so-important.html.

287 Kathleen Romig and Kathleen Bryant, "A National Paid Leave Program Would Help Workers, Families," April 27, 2021, https://www.cbpp.org/research/economy/a-national-paid-leave-program-would-help-workers-families.

288 Melissa S. Kearney and Phillip B. Levine, "The Consequences and Causes of Declining US Fertility," The Aspen Economic Strategy Group, August 13, 2022, https://www.economicstrategygroup.org/publication/kearney_levine/.

289 Peter McDonald, "Sustaining Fertility through Public Policy: The Range of Options," *Population* 57, no. 3(2002): 417–446.

290 David G. Smith and W. Brad Johnson, "Gender Equity Starts in the Home," May 4, 2020, *Harvard Business Review*, https://hbr.org/2020/05/gender-equity-starts-in-the-home.

291 Chris Kolmar, "20+ Essential US Paid Family Leave Statistics [2022]: Quick Facts and Findings," October 31, 2022, https://www.zippia.com/advice/paid-family-leave-statistics/.

292 Tomáš Sobotka, Anna Matysiak, and Zuzanna Brzozowska., "Policy Responses to Low Fertility: How Effective Are They?" United Nations Population Fund, May 2019, https://www.unfpa.org/sites/default/files/pub-pdf/Policy_responses_low_fertility_UNFPA_WP_Final_corrections_7Feb2020_CLEAN.pdf.

293 Peter McDonald, "Sustaining Fertility through Public Policy: The Range of Options," *Population* 57, no. 3(2002): 417–446.

294 Darrell Bricker and John Ibbitson, *Empty Planet: The Shock of Global Population Decline* (New York: Crown Publishing, 2019).

295 "Fact Sheet: Childcare Prices in Local Areas," U.S. Department of Labor Women's Bureau, January 2023, https://www.dol.gov/sites/dolgov/files/WB/NDCP/WB-fact-sheet-NDCP.pdf.

296 Mark Lino, "The Cost of Raising a Child," USDA, February 18, 2020, https://www.usda.gov/media/blog/2017/01/13/cost-raising-child.

297 Institute of Education Sciences National Center for Education Statistics. 2021. Average Undergraduate Tuition, Fees, Room, and Board Rates Charged for Full-Time Students in Degree-Granting Postsecondary Institutions, by Level and Control of Institution: Selected Years, 1963-64 Through 2020-21. https://nces.ed.gov/programs/digest/d21/tables/dt21_330.10.asp.

298 Jonathan V. Last, *What to Expect When No One's Expecting: America's Coming Demographic Disaster* (New York: Encounter Books, 2013).

299 Melissa S. Kearney and Phillip B. Levine, "The Consequences and Causes of Declining US Fertility," The Aspen Economic Strategy Group, August 13, 2022, https://www.economicstrategygroup.org/publication/kearney_levine/.

300 Alexandra Stevenson, "China Offers Women Perks for Having Babies. Single Moms Don't Quality," *New York Times*, July 6, 2022, https://www.nytimes.com/2022/07/06/business/economy/china-reproductive-rights-women.html.

301 Sam Kim, "Korea to Triple Baby Payments After It Smashes Own Record for World's Lowest Fertility Rate," Bloomberg, August 30, 2022, https://www.bloomberg.com/news/articles/2022-08-31/korea-to-triple-baby-payments-in-bid-to-tackle-fertility-crisis?leadSource=uverify%20wall.

302 Shaun Walker, "'Baby Machines': Eastern Europe's Answer to Depopulation," March 4, 2020, https://www.theguardian.com/world/2020/mar/04/baby-bonuses-fit-the-nationalist-agenda-but-do-they-work.

303 Jessica Grose, "If We Want More Babies, Our 'Profoundly Anti-Family' System Needs an Overhaul," *New York Times*, March 8, 2023, https://www.nytimes.com/2023/03/08/opinion/birth-rate.html.

304 Shaun Walker and Flora Garamvolgyi, "Viktor Orbán Sparks Outrage with Attack on 'Race Mixing' in Europe," July 4, 2022, https://www.theguardian.com/world/2022/jul/24/viktor-orban-against-race-mixing-europe-hungary.

305 Cyrielle Cabot, "Population Decline in Russia: 'Putin Has No Choice but to Win' in Ukraine," May 24, 2022, https://www.france24.com/en/europe/20220524-population-decline-in-russia-putin-has-no-other-choice-but-to-win-in-ukraine.

306 Shaun Walker, "'Baby Machines': Eastern Europe's Answer to Depopulation," March 4, 2020, https://www.theguardian.com/world/2020/mar/04/baby-bonuses-fit-the-nationalist-agenda-but-do-they-work.

307 Cyrielle Cabot, "Population Decline in Russia: 'Putin Has No Choice but to Win' in Ukraine," May 24, 2022, https://www.france24.com/en/europe/20220524-population-decline-in-russia-putin-has-no-other-choice-but-to-win-in-ukraine.

308 Jonathan V. Last, *What to Expect When No One's Expecting: America's Coming Demographic Disaster* (New York: Encounter Books, 2013).

309 Gearoid Reidy, "The Fertility Crisis Started in Japan, But It Won't Stay There," June 22, 2022, https://www.washingtonpost.com/business/the-fertility-crisis-started-in-japan-butit-wont-stay-there/2022/06/21/8c343abe-f19d-11ec-ac16-8fbf7194cd78_story.html.

310 United Nations Population Fund, "Shrinking Populations in Eastern Europe," UNFPA, n.d., https://eeca.unfpa.org/sites/default/files/pub-pdf/Shrinking%20population_low%20fertility%20QA.pdf.

311 Jan Hoem, "The Impact of Public Policies on European Fertility," *Demographic Research* 19, no. 10 (2008): 249–260, https://www.demographic-research.org/volumes/vol19/10/19-10.pdf.

312 Jessica Grose, "If We Want More Babies, Our 'Profoundly Anti-Family' System Needs an Overhaul," *New York Times*, March 8, 2023, https://www.nytimes.com/2023/03/08/opinion/birth-rate.html.

313 Grose, "If We Want More Babies."

314 Samantha Selinger-Morris, "Artificial Wombs and Gene Editing: What Are the New Frontiers in IVF?," October 30, 2022, https://www.smh.com.au/lifestyle/health-and-wellness/artificial-wombs-and-gene-editing-what-are-the-new-frontiers-in-ivf-20220609-p5asoc.html.

315 Gina Kolata, "Scientists Grow Mouse Embryos in a Mechanical Womb," March 17, 2021, https://www.nytimes.com/2021/03/17/health/mice-artificial-uterus.html?referringSource=articleShare.

316 Shaun Walker, "'Baby Machines': Eastern Europe's Answer to Depopulation," March 4, 2020, https://www.theguardian.com/world/2020/mar/04/baby-bonuses-fit-the-nationalist-agenda-but-do-they-work.

317 Jessica Grose, "If We Want More Babies, Our 'Profoundly Anti-Family' System Needs an Overhaul," *New York Times*, March 8, 2023, https://www.nytimes.com/2023/03/08/opinion/birth-rate.html.

318 Shaun Walker, "'Baby Machines': Eastern Europe's Answer to Depopulation," March 4, 2020, https://www.theguardian.com/world/2020/mar/04/baby-bonuses-fit-the-nationalist-agenda-but-do-they-work.

319 Sam Kim, "Korea to Triple Baby Payments After It Smashes Own Record for World's Lowest Fertility Rate," August 30, 2022, https://www.bloomberg.com/news/articles/2022-08-31/korea-to-triple-baby-payments-in-bid-to-tackle-fertility-crisis?leadSource=uverify%20wall.

320 "World Population Prospects 2022: Summary of Results," United Nations Department of Economic and Social Affairs, July 2022, https://www.un.org/development/desa/pd/sites/www.un.org.development.desa.pd/files/undesa_pd_2022_wpp_key-messages.pdf.

321 United Nations Population Fund, "Shrinking Populations in Eastern Europe," UNFPA, n.d., https://eeca.unfpa.org/sites/default/files/pub-pdf/Shrinking%20population_low%20fertility%20QA.pdf.

322 Emil Vollset et al., "Fertility, Mortality, Migration, and Population Scenarios for 195 Countries and Territories from 2017 to 2011: A Forecasting Analysis for the Global Burden of Disease Study," *Lancet* 396, no. 10258 (2020): 1285–1306, https://www.thelancet.com/journals/lancet/article/PIIS0140-6736(20)30677-2/fulltext.

323 Fred Pearce, *The Coming Population Crash: and Our Planet's Surprising Future* (Boston: Beacon Press, 2010).

324 Emil Vollset et al., "Fertility, Mortality, Migration, and Population Scenarios for 195 Countries and Territories from 2017 to 2011: A Forecasting Analysis for the Global Burden of Disease Study," *Lancet* 396, no. 10258 (2020): 1285–1306, https://www.thelancet.com/journals/lancet/article/PIIS0140-6736(20)30677-2/fulltext.

325 Michael Herrmann, "The Global Population Will Soon Reach 8 Billion— Then What?" United Nations, July 11, 2022, https://www.un.org/en/un-chronicle/global-population-will-soon-reach-8-billion-then-what.

326 Christian Shepherd, "China's First Population Decline in 60 Years Sounds Demographic Alarm," *Washington Post*, January 17, 2023, https://www.washingtonpost.com/world/2023/01/17/china-population-shrinking-decline-crisis/?utm_campaign=wp_post_most&utm_medium=email&utm_source=newsletter&wpisrc=nl_most&carta-url=https%3A%2F%2Fs2.washingtonpost.com%2Fcar-ln-tr%2F38df9ca%2F63c6d31def9bf6.

327 Michael Herrmann, "The Global Population Will Soon Reach 8 Billion— Then What?" United Nations, July 11, 2022, https://www.un.org/en/un-chronicle/global-population-will-soon-reach-8-billion-then-what.

328 Murray, Stephanie H. 2021. *How Low Can America's Birth Rate Go Before It's a Problem?* June 9. https://fivethirtyeight.com/features/how-low-can-americas-birth-rate-go-before-its-a-problem/.

329 Murray, Stephanie H. 2021. *How Low Can America's Birth Rate Go Before It's a Problem?* June 9. https://fivethirtyeight.com/features/how-low-can-americas-birth-rate-go-before-its-a-problem/.

330 United Nations Population Fund, "Shrinking Populations in Eastern Europe," UNFPA, n.d., https://eeca.unfpa.org/sites/default/files/pub-pdf/Shrinking%20population_low%20fertility%20QA.pdf.

Chapter 8

331 Charles Goodhart and Manoj Pradhan, *The Great Demographic Reversal: Ageing Societies, Waning Inequality, and an Inflation Revival* (London: Springer Nature, 2020).

332 Diamond, Jared. 2013. *How Societies Can Grow Old Better.* https://www. ted.com/talks/jared_diamond_how_societies_can_grow_old_better/ transcript.

333 N. K. Chadha, "Intergenerational Relationships: An Indian Perspective," United Nations, n.d., https://www.un.org/esa/socdev/family/ docs/egm12/CHADHA.PAPER.pdf.

334 Mark E. Williams, "Growing Old in Ancient Greek and Rome," April 2, 2017, https://www.psychologyto-day.com/us/blog/the-art-and-science-aging-well/201704/ growing-old-in-ancient-greece-and-rome.

335 Thomas R. Cole, "The 'Enlightened' View of Aging: Victorian Morality in a New Key." *The Hastings Center Report* 13 no. 3(1983): 34–40.

336 Karina Martinez Carter, "How the Elderly Are Treated Around the World," January 10, 2015, https://theweek.com/articles/462230/ how-elderly-are-treated-around-world.

337 Jared Diamond, "How Societies Can Grow Old Better," 2013 https://www. ted.com/talks/jared_diamond_how_societies_can_grow_old_better/ transcript.

338 National Academies of Sciences, Engineering, and Medicine, *Understanding the Aging Workforce: Defining a Research Agenda* (Washington, DC: The National Academies Press, 2022).

339 Thomas R. Cole, "The 'Enlightened' View of Aging: Victorian Morality in a New Key." *The Hastings Center Report* 13 no. 3(1983): 34–40.

340 Robert N Butler, "Ageism," in *The Encyclopedia of Aging Fourth Edition*, ed. Richard Schulz, Linda S. Noelker, Kenneth Rockwood, and Richard L. Sprott (New York: Springer Publishing Company, 2006), 41–42.

341 National Academies of Sciences, Engineering, and Medicine, *Understanding the Aging Workforce: Defining a Research Agenda* (Washington, DC: The National Academies Press, 2022).

342 Thomas R. Cole, "The 'Enlightened' View of Aging: Victorian Morality in a New Key." *The Hastings Center Report* 13 no. 3(1983): 34–40.

343 Jere Daniel, "Learning to Love Growing Old," September 1, 1994, https://www.psychologytoday.com/intl/articles/199409/learning-love-growing-old.

344 Hanne Laceulle, "Aging and Self-Realization: Cultural Narratives about Later Life" (Bielefeld: Transcript Verlag, 2018).

345 Jared Diamond, "How Societies Can Grow Old Better," TED, 2013, https://www.ted.com/talks/jared_diamond_how_societies_can_grow_old_better/transcript.

346 Diamond, "Societies."

347 Diamond, "Societies."

348 Paul B. Baltes and Ursula M. Staudinger, "Wisdom: A Metaheuristic (Pragmatic) to Orchestrate Mind and Virtue Toward Excellence," *American Psychologist*, 2000, https://library.mpib-berlin.mpg.de/ft/pb/PB_Wisdom_2000.pdf.

349 Kerry Hannon, "Is It Time to Abolish Mandatory Retirement?" *Forbes*, August 2, 2015, https://www.forbes.com/sites/nextavenue/2015/08/02/is-it-time-to-abolish-mandatory-retirement/?sh=514513d640db.

350 Alana Officer and Vânia de la Fuente-Núñez, "A Global Campaign to Combat Ageism," *Bulletin of the World Health Organization* 96

no. 4(2018): 295–296. https://www.ncbi.nlm.nih.gov/pmc/articles/PMC5872010/#R14.

351 Jere Daniel, "Learning to Love Growing Old," September 1, 1994, https://www.psychologytoday.com/intl/articles/199409/learning-love-growing-old.

352 Daniel, "Growing Old."

353 Daniel, "Growing Old."

354 Stephen Mihm, "Ready to Work Until You Die? America Needs You," September 8, 2022, https://www.bloomberg.com/opinion/articles/2022-09-08/ready-to-work-until-you-die-america-needs-you?leadSource=uverify%20wall.

355 D. G. Smith, "What Is the Ideal Retirement Age for Your Health?" *New York Times*, April 3, 2023, https://www.nytimes.com/2023/04/03/well/live/retirement-age-health.html.

356 Peter Feuerherd, "Why Retirement Age Is 65 (And Why It's Getting Higher)," May 8, 2017, https://daily.jstor.org/why-retirement-is-age-65-and-why-its-getting-higher/.

357 "Life Expectancy of the World Population," Worldometer, n.d., https://www.worldometers.info/demographics/life-expectancy/.

358 "2021 Profile of Older Americans," Administration for Community Living, 2022, https://acl.gov/sites/default/files/Profile%20of%20OA/2021%20Profile%20of%20OA/2021ProfileOlderAmericans_508.pdf.

359 "Life Expectancy of the World Population," Worldometer, n.d., https://www.worldometers.info/demographics/life-expectancy/.

360 "Pensions at a Glance: OECD and G20 Indicators," OECD, n.d., https://www.oecd-ilibrary.org/sites/a957e891-en/index.html?itemId=/content/component/a957e891-en.

361 Jerome H Powell, "Inflation and the Labor Market," November 30, 2022, https://www.federalreserve.gov/newsevents/speech/powell20221130a.htm.

362 Eshe Nelson, "Britain Wants Its Early Retirees Back, but Their Days Are 'Never Boring,'" March 14, 2023, https://www.nytimes.com/2023/03/14/business/britain-retirees-return-to-work-covid.html.

363 The Board of Trustees, Federal Old-Age and Survivors Insurance and Federal Disability Insurance Trust Funds, "The 2022 Annual Report of the Board of Trustees of the Federal Old-Age and Survivors Insurance and Federal Disability Insurance Trust Funds," Social Security, 2022, https://www.ssa.gov/oact/TR/2022/tr2022.pdf.

364 Social Security, "Federal Disability Insurance Trust Funds."

365 "A Summary of the 2022 Annual Reports," Social Security and Medicare Boards of Trustees, n.d., https://www.ssa.gov/oact/TRSUM/index.html.

366 National Academies of Sciences, Engineering, and Medicine, *Understanding the Aging Workforce: Defining a Research Agenda* (Washington, DC: The National Academies Press, 2022).

367 L. C. Hawkley, M. Kozloski, and J. Wong, "A Profile of Social Connectedness in Older Adults," 2017, https://connect2affect.org/wp-content/uploads/2020/06/A-Profile-of-Social-Connectedness-1-1.pdf.

368 National Academies of Sciences, Engineering, and Medicine. n.d. "Social Isolation and Loneliness in Older Adults: Opportunities for the Health Care System." *National Academies Press.* https://nap.nationalacademies.org/read/25663/chapter/1.

369 National Academies of Sciences, Engineering, and Medicine, *Understanding the Aging Workforce: Defining a Research Agenda* (Washington, DC: The National Academies Press, 2022).

370 Dave Bernard, "Why 65 Is Too Young to Retire," October 18, 2013, https://money.usnews.com/money/blogs/on-retirement/2013/10/18/why-65-is-too-young-to-retire.

371 Bernard, "Retire."

372 Liz Alderman, "As France Moves to Delay Retirement, Older Workers Are in a Quandary," *New York Times*, January 23, 2023, https://www.nytimes.com/2023/01/17/business/france-retirement-age-pension.html.

373 Jack Kelly, "More Than Half of U.S. Workers Are Unhappy in Their Jobs: Here's What Needs to Be Done Now," October 25, 2019. https://www.forbes.com/sites/jackkelly/2019/10/25/more-than-half-of-us-workers-are-unhappy-in-their-jobs-heres-why-and-what-needs-to-be-done-now/?sh=73eb3ba12024.

374 Neil Irwin and Quoctrung Bui, "The Rich Live Longer Everywhere. For the Poor, Geography Matters," April 11, 2016, https://www.nytimes.com/interactive/2016/04/11/upshot/for-the-poor-geography-is-life-and-death.html.

375 Eshe Nelson, "Britain Wants Its Early Retirees Back, but Their Days Are 'Never Boring,'" March 14, 2023, https://www.nytimes.com/2023/03/14/business/britain-retirees-return-to-work-covid.html.

376 Fred Pearce, *The Coming Population Crash: and Our Planet's Surprising Future* (Boston: Beacon Press, 2010).

377 National Academies of Sciences, Engineering, and Medicine, *Understanding the Aging Workforce: Defining a Research Agenda* (Washington, DC: The National Academies Press, 2022).

378 "The Benefits of Intergenerational Mentoring," Positive Maturity, May 19, 2020, https://www.positivematurity.org/the-benefits-of-intergenerational-mentoring/.

379 National Academies of Sciences, Engineering, and Medicine, *Understanding the Aging Workforce: Defining a Research Agenda* (Washington, DC: The National Academies Press, 2022).

380 Daniela J. Lamas, "As a Doctor, I See Aging Differently," *New York Times*, January 4, 2023, https://www.nytimes.com/2023/01/04/opinion/anti-aging-science-longevity.html?smid=em-share.

381 "Aging in Place: Facilitating Choice and Independence," Evidence Matters, 2013, https://www.huduser.gov/portal/periodicals/em/fall13/highlight1.html.

382 Charles Goodhart and Manoj Pradhan, *The Great Demographic Reversal: Ageing Societies, Waning Inequality, and an Inflation Revival* (London: Springer Nature, 2020).

383 "Dementia Statistics," Alzheimer's Disease International, n.d., https://www.alzint.org/about/dementia-facts-figures/dementia-statistics/.

384 Charles Goodhart and Manoj Pradhan, *The Great Demographic Reversal: Ageing Societies, Waning Inequality, and an Inflation Revival* (London: Springer Nature, 2020).

385 Motoko Rich and Hida Hikari, "A Yale Professor Suggested Mass Suicide for Old People in Japan. What Did He Mean?," February 12, 2023, https://www.nytimes.com/2023/02/12/world/asia/japan-elderly-mass-suicide.html.

386 Bonnie Clipper, *Building a Culture of Innovation and Reconstructing Nursing Practice* (Indianapolis: Sigma, 2023).

387 National Academies of Sciences, Engineering, and Medicine, *Understanding the Aging Workforce: Defining a Research Agenda* (Washington, DC: The National Academies Press, 2022).

388 National Academies of Sciences, Engineering, and Medicine, *Understanding*.

389 National Academies of Sciences, Engineering, and Medicine, *Understanding*.

Chapter 9

390 Nicholas Eberstadt, "Can America Cope with Demographic Decline?," American Enterprise Institute, October 6, 2021, https://www.aei.org/articles/can-america-cope-with-demographic-decline/.

391 Emil Vollset et al., "Fertility, Mortality, Migration, and Population Scenarios for 195 Countries and Territories from 2017 to 2011: A Forecasting Analysis for the Global Burden of Disease Study," *Lancet* 396, no. 10258 (2020): 1285–1306, https://www.thelancet.com/journals/lancet/article/PIIS0140-6736(20)30677-2/fulltext.

392 UN Population Division Data Portal, United Nations Population Division, 2022, https://population.un.org/dataportal/data/indicators/19/locations/156/start/1950/end/2022/table/pivotbylocation.

393 Gebeloff Robert, Dana Goldstein, and Winnie Hu. "U.S. Population Ticks Up, but the Rate of Growth Stays Near Historic Lows," December 22, 2022, https://www.nytimes.com/2022/12/22/us/census-population.html.

394 Jonathan V. Last, *What to Expect When No One's Expecting: America's Coming Demographic Disaster* (New York: Encounter Books, 2013).

395 Fred Pearce, *The Coming Population Crash: and Our Planet's Surprising Future* (Boston: Beacon Press, 2010).

396 Darrell Bricker and John Ibbitson, *Empty Planet: The Shock of Global Population Decline* (New York: Crown Publishing, 2019).

397 Fred Pearce, *The Coming Population Crash: and Our Planet's Surprising Future* (Boston: Beacon Press, 2010).

398 Kenneth Johnson, "Rural America Lost Population over the Past Decade for the First Time in History," February 22, 2022, https://carsey.unh.edu/publication-rural-america-lost-population-over-past-decade-for-first-time-in-history.

399 Robert Gebeloff, Dana Goldstein, and Winnie Hu, "Cities Lost Population in 2021, Leading to the Slowest Year of Growth in U.S. History," *New York Times*, March 24, 2022, https://www.nytimes.com/2022/03/24/us/census-2021-population-growth.html.

400 Derek Thompson, "The Doom Loop of Modern Liberalism," October 24, 2017, https://www.theatlantic.com/business/archive/2017/10/immigration-modern-liberalism/543744/.

401 Darrell Bricker and John Ibbitson, *Empty Planet: The Shock of Global Population Decline* (New York: Crown Publishing, 2019).

402 Shikha Dalmia, "Who Has the Cure for America's Declining Birth Rate? Canada," August 18, 2021, https://www.nytimes.com/2021/08/18/opinion/us-canada-immigration.html.

403 Paul Krugman, "How Immigrants Are Saving the Economy," *New York Times*, April 13, 2023, https://www.nytimes.com/2023/04/13/opinion/how-immigrants-are-saving-the-economy.html.

404 "Age Dependency Ratio, Old (% of Working-Age Population)," Our World in Data, n.d., https://ourworldindata.org/search?q=old+age+dependency+ratio.

405 Stuart Anderson, "Immigrants and Billion-Dollar Companies," National Foundation for American Policy, October 2018, https://nfap.com/wp-content/uploads/2019/03/2018-BILLION-DOLLAR-STARTUPS.NFAP-Policy-Brief.2018.pdf.

406 Paul Krugman, "How Immigrants Are Saving the Economy," *New York Times*, April 13, 2023, https://www.nytimes.com/2023/04/13/opinion/how-immigrants-are-saving-the-economy.html.

407 Emil Vollset et al., "Fertility, Mortality, Migration, and Population Scenarios for 195 Countries and Territories from 2017 to 2011: A Forecasting Analysis for the Global Burden of Disease Study," *Lancet* 396, no. 10258 (2020): 1285–1306, https://www.thelancet.com/journals/lancet/article/PIIS0140-6736(20)30677-2/fulltext.

408 Nicholas Riccardi, "Less Immigrant Labor in US contributing to Price Hikes," Associated Press, May 7, 2022, https://apnews.com/article/immigration-covid-health-business-united-states-dcfd75981dcd212e-f6747eeaf87f4f31.

409 Emil Vollset et al., "Fertility, Mortality, Migration, and Population Scenarios for 195 Countries and Territories from 2017 to 2011: A Forecasting Analysis for the Global Burden of Disease Study," *Lancet* 396, no. 10258 (2020): 1285–1306, https://www.thelancet.com/journals/lancet/article/PIIS0140-6736(20)30677-2/fulltext.

410 "What Is Populism?" *Economist*, December 19, 2016, https://www.economist.com/the-economist-explains/2016/12/19/what-is-populism.

411 Derek Thompson, "The Doom Loop of Modern Liberalism," October 24, 2017, https://www.theatlantic.com/business/archive/2017/10/immigration-modern-liberalism/543744/.

412 Krisztina Than, "Hungary's Orban Says His Anti-Immigration Stance Not Rooted in Racism After Backlash," Reuters, July 28, 2022, https://

www.reuters.com/world/europe/hungarys-orban-says-his-anti-immigration-stance-not-rooted-racism-after-backlash-2022-07-28/.

413 "Migrant Crisis: Finland's Case Against Immigration," BBC, September 9, 2015, https://www.bbc.com/news/world-europe-34185297.

414 Jason Horowitz, "The Double Whammy Making Italy the West's Fastest-Shrinking Nation," *New York Times*, January 30, 2023, https://www.nytimes.com/2023/01/30/world/europe/italy-birthrate.html.

415 Janet Adamy and Paul Overberg, "Places Most Unsettled by Rapid Demographic Change Are Drawn to Donald Trump," November 1, 2016, https://www.wsj.com/articles/places-most-unsettled-by-rapid-demographic-change-go-for-donald-trump-1478010940.

416 Philip Auerswald and Joon Yun, "As Population Growth Slows, Populism Surges, May 22, 2018, https://www.nytimes.com/2018/05/22/opinion/populist-populism-fertility-rates.html.

417 Olga Khazan, "A Surprising Reason to Worry about Low Birth Rates, May 26, 2018, https://www.theatlantic.com/health/archive/2018/05/a-surprising-reason-to-worry-about-low-birth-rates/561308/.

418 Darrell Bricker and John Ibbitson, *Empty Planet: The Shock of Global Population Decline* (New York: Crown Publishing, 2019).

419 Urban Dictionary, *Schrödinger's Immigrant*, n.d., https://www.urban-dictionary.com/define.php?term=Schr%C3%B6dinger%27s%20Immigrant.

420 Jessica Love, "Immigrants to the U.S. Create More Jobs Than They Take," October 5, 2020, https://insight.kellogg.northwestern.edu/article/immigrants-to-the-u-s-create-more-jobs-than-they-take.

421 Bruce Thornton, "America's Problem of Assimilation," May 24, 2012, https://www.hoover.org/research/americas-problem-assimilation#.

422 Darrell Bricker and John Ibbitson, *Empty Planet: The Shock of Global Population Decline* (New York: Crown Publishing, 2019).

423 Jonathan V. Last, *What to Expect When No One's Expecting: America's Coming Demographic Disaster* (New York: Encounter Books, 2013).

424 UN Population Division Data Portal, United Nations Population Division, 2022, https://population.un.org/dataportal/data/indicators/19/locations/156/start/1950/end/2022/table/pivotbylocation.

425 Data Portal, United Nations Population Division.

426 Data Portal, United Nations Population Division.

427 Jonathan V. Last, *What to Expect When No One's Expecting: America's Coming Demographic Disaster* (New York: Encounter Books, 2013).

428 Lopez, Oscar, and Maria Abi-Habib. 2022. *Ending a Decade-Long Decline, More Mexicans Are Migrating to U.S.* July 1. https://www.nytimes.com/2022/07/01/world/americas/migrants-mexico-texas.html.

429 Shikha Dalmia, "Who Has the Cure for America's Declining Birth Rate? Canada," August 18, 2021, https://www.nytimes.com/2021/08/18/opinion/us-canada-immigration.html.

430 Spencer Van Dyk, "Canada Welcomed Record Number of Immigrants in 2022," January 3, 2023, https://www.ctvnews.ca/politics/canada-welcomed-record-number-of-immigrants-in-2022-1.6216022.

431 Amelia Cheatham, "What Is Canada's Immigration Policy?," February 9, 2022, https://www.cfr.org/backgrounder/what-canadas-immigration-policy.

432 Norimitsu Onishi, "How a Town Famous for Xenophobia Fell in Love with Immigrants," December 17, 2022. https://www.nytimes.com/2022/12/17/world/canada/quebec-immigrants-xenophobia.html.

433 Philip Auerswald and Joon Yun, "As Population Growth Slows, Populism Surges, May 22, 2018, https://www.nytimes.com/2018/05/22/opinion/populist-populism-fertility-rates.html.

434 Kristie De Peña, Robert Leonard, and David Oman, "Over 75,000 Job Openings in Iowa Alone. Millions of Refugees Seeking Work. Make the Connection," February 2, 2023, https://www.nytimes.com/2023/02/02/opinion/immigration-states.html.

435 Jonathan V. Last, *What to Expect When No One's Expecting: America's Coming Demographic Disaster* (New York: Encounter Books, 2013).

436 Fred Pearce, *The Coming Population Crash: and Our Planet's Surprising Future* (Boston: Beacon Press, 2010).

437 Pearce, *The Coming Population Crash*.

438 Tom Fairless, "Germany Is Short of Workers, but Its Migrants Are Struggling to Find Jobs," December 12, 2022, https://www.wsj.com/articles/germany-is-short-of-workers-but-its-migrants-are-struggling-to-find-jobs-11670844930?st=r04535yny46wopa&reflink=desktopwebshare_permalink.

439 Kai McNamee, "Migration Could Prevent a Looming Population Crisis. But There Are Catches," January 27, 2023, https://www.npr.org/2023/01/27/1151734308/immigration-economy-birth-rate-population.

440 McNamee, "Migration."

441 Rick Gladstone, "World Population Could Peak Decades Ahead of U.N. Forecast, Study Asserts," *New York Times*, July 14, 2020, https://www.nytimes.com/2020/07/14/world/americas/

global-population-trends.html#:~:text=The%20study%2C%20
published%20in%20The%20Lancet%2C%20said%20
an,shrink%20by%20more%20than%2050%20percent%20by%20
2100.?msclkid=967b02e6bcef11ecb74f365ff65ff4f4.

Chapter 10

442 Wolfgang Fengler, Homi Kharas, and Juan Caballero, "The Forgotten 3 Billion," October 21, 2022, https://www.brookings.edu/blog/future-development/2022/10/21/the-forgotten-3-billion/.

443 "The World Has Made Great Progress in Eradicating Extreme Poverty," *Economist*, March 30, 2017, https://www.economist.com/international/2017/03/30/the-world-has-made-great-progress-in-eradicating-extreme-poverty?utm_medium=cpc.adword.pd&utm_source=google&ppccampaignID=17210591673&ppcadID=&utm_campaign=a.22brand_pmax&utm_content=conversion.direct-res.

444 Anthony B. Kim and Patrick Tyrrell, "Economic Freedom Enables Great Escape from Poverty," February 13, 2018, https://www.heritage.org/poverty-and-inequality/commentary/economic-freedom-enables-great-escape-poverty.

445 Arthur Brooks, "A Conservative's Plea: Let's Work Together," TED, 2016, https://www.ted.com/talks/arthur_brooks_a_conservative_s_plea_let_s_work_together.

446 Brooks, "A Conservative's Plea."

447 Juliana Mesasce Horowitz, "Despite Challenges at Home and Work, Most Working Moms and Dads Say Being Employed Is What's Best for Them," September 12, 2019, https://www.pewresearch.org/fact-tank/2019/09/12/despite-challenges-at-home-and-work-most-working-moms-and-dads-say-being-employed-is-whats-best-for-them/.

448 Yuval Noah Harari, *Sapiens: A Brief History of Humankind* (New York: Harper Collins Publishers, 2015).

449 "Family Responsibilities Discrimination," Workplace Fairness, n.d., https://www.workplacefairness.org/family-responsibilities-discrimination.

450 Joan C. Williams and Amy J. C. Cuddy, "Will Working Mothers Take Your Company to Court?," *Harvard Business Review*, September 2012, https://hbr.org/2012/09/will-working-mothers-take-your-company-to-court.

451 Jonathan V. Last, *What to Expect When No One's Expecting: America's Coming Demographic Disaster* (New York: Encounter Books, 2013).

452 Peter McDonald, "Sustaining Fertility through Public Policy: The Range of Options," *Population* 57, no. 3(2002): 417–446.

453 Jonathan V. Last, *What to Expect When No One's Expecting: America's Coming Demographic Disaster* (New York: Encounter Books, 2013).

454 Adam Hickman and Jennifer Robison, "Is Working Remotely Effective? Gallup Research Says Yes," Gallup, January 24, 2020, https://www.gallup.com/workplace/283985/working-remotely-effective-gallup-research-says-yes.aspx.

455 National Academies of Sciences, Engineering, and Medicine, *Understanding the Aging Workforce: Defining a Research Agenda* (Washington, DC: The National Academies Press, 2022).

456 Nicholas Eberstadt, "Can America Cope with Demographic Decline?," American Enterprise Institute, October 6, 2021, https://www.aei.org/articles/can-america-cope-with-demographic-decline/.

457 National Academies of Sciences, Engineering, and Medicine, *Understanding the Aging Workforce: Defining a Research Agenda* (Washington, DC: The National Academies Press, 2022).

458 National Academies of Sciences, Engineering, and Medicine, *Understanding*.

459 Fred Pearce, *The Coming Population Crash: and Our Planet's Surprising Future* (Boston: Beacon Press, 2010).

460 National Academies of Sciences, Engineering, and Medicine, *Understanding the Aging Workforce: Defining a Research Agenda* (Washington, DC: The National Academies Press, 2022).

461 "Survey: Companies Struggle to Hire and Promote Amid Uptick in Delayed Retirements," Nationwide Retirement Institute, September 28, 2022, https://news.nationwide.com/companies-struggle-to-hire-promote-amid-uptick-in-delayed-retirements/.

462 Roberta Kwok, "Younger Workers Lose Out When Their Coworkers Delay Retirement," Kellogg Insight, June 1, 2020, https://insight.kellogg.northwestern.edu/article/retirement-delays-impact-younger-workers.

463 Nicole Maestras et al., "Working Conditions in the United States: Results of the 2015 American Working Conditions Survey," Rand, 2017, https://www.rand.org/pubs/research_reports/RR2014.html.

464 Rutger Bregman, "A Growing Number of People Think Their Job Is Useless. Time to Rethink the Meaning of Work," World Economic Forum, April 12, 2017, https://www.weforum.org/agenda/2017/04/why-its-time-to-rethink-the-meaning-of-work.

465 Will Dahlgreen. "37% of British Workers Think Their Jobs Are Meaningless," YouGov, August 12, 2015, https://yougov.co.uk/topics/society/articles-reports/2015/08/12/british-jobs-meaningless.

466 Jack Kelly, "More Than Half of U.S. Workers Are Unhappy in Their Jobs: Here's What Needs to Be Done Now," *Forbes*, October 25, 2019, https://www.forbes.com/sites/jackkelly/2019/10/25/more-than-half-of-us-workers-are-unhappy-in-their-jobs-heres-why-and-what-needs-to-be-done-now/?sh=73eb3ba12024.

467 Charles Goodhart and Manoj Pradhan, *The Great Demographic Reversal: Ageing Societies, Waning Inequality, and an Inflation Revival* (London: Springer Nature, 2020).

468 "Will Robots Really Steal Our Jobs?" PWC, 2018, https://www.pwc.co.uk/services/economics/insights/the-impact-of-automation-on-jobs.html.

469 A. W. Geiger, "How Americans See Automation and the Workplace in 7 Charts," April 18, 2019, https://www.pewresearch.org/fact-tank/2019/04/08/how-americans-see-automation-and-the-workplace-in-7-charts/.

470 Charles Goodhart and Manoj Pradhan, *The Great Demographic Reversal: Ageing Societies, Waning Inequality, and an Inflation Revival* (London: Springer Nature, 2020).

471 John Yoon, "South Korea Breaks Record for World's Lowest Fertility Rate, Again" August 24, 2022, https://www.nytimes.com/2022/08/24/world/asia/south-korea-fertility-rate.html.

472 "What Skills Does the Future Workforce Need?," Boston Consulting Group. March 18, 2016.

473 Charles Goodhart and Manoj Pradhan, *The Great Demographic Reversal: Ageing Societies, Waning Inequality, and an Inflation Revival* (London: Springer Nature, 2020).

474 "What Skills Does the Future Workforce Need?," Boston Consulting Group. March 18, 2016.

475 Boston Consulting Group, "Skills."

476 Boston Consulting Group, "Skills."

477 "Short-Termism," CFA Institute, n.d. https://www.cfainstitute.org/en/advocacy/issues/short-termism#sort=%40pubbrowsedate%20descending.

478 J. Randall Woodridge, "Competitive Decline and Corporate Restructuring: Is a Myopic Stock Market to Blame?" *Journal of Applied Corporate Finance* 1, no. 1(1988): 26–36.

479 Woodridge, "Competitive Decline."

480 Peter Drucker, "A Crisis of Capitalism," *Wall Street Journal* 30 (1986): 30–31.

481 Dominic Barton, James Manyika, and Sarah Keohane Williamson, "Finally, Evidence That Managing for the Long Term Pays Off," *Harvard Business Review*, February 7, 2017, https://hbr.org/2017/02/finally-proof-that-managing-for-the-long-term-pays-off.

482 Barton, Manyika, and Williamson, "Long Term."

483 Barton, Manyika, and Williamson, "Long Term."

Conclusion

484 UN Population Division Data Portal, United Nations Population Division, 2022, https://population.un.org/dataportal/data/indicators/19/locations/156/start/1950/end/2022/table/pivotbylocation.

485 Data Portal, United Nations Population Division.

486 Wang Feng, "The Alternative, Optimistic Story of Population Decline," January 30, 2023, *New York Times*, https://www.nytimes.com/2023/01/30/opinion/china-world-population-decline.html.

487 Nicholas Eberstadt, "Can America Cope with Demographic Decline?,"
     American Enterprise Institute, October 6, 2021, https://www.aei.org/
     articles/can-america-cope-with-demographic-decline/.

Printed in the USA
CPSIA information can be obtained
at www.ICGtesting.com
JSHW081448151123
52143JS00014B/228/J